A Journey into
Flaubert's
Normandy

D1315145

ArtPlace Series

Roaring Forties Press
1053 Santa Fe Avenue
Berkeley, California 94706

ISBN 0-9766706-8-2

Library of Congress Cataloging-in-Publication Data
Patton, Susannah, 1964-
    A journey into Flaubert's Normandy / Susannah Patton.
       p. cm. -- (ArtPlace series)
    Includes bibliographical references and index.
    ISBN 0-9766706-8-2
    1. Flaubert, Gustave, 1821-1880—Homes and haunts—France—Normandy. 2. Authors,
French—Homes and haunts—France—Normandy. 3. Normandy (France)—Intellectual life—
19th century. 4. Normandy (France)—In literature. 5. Normandy (France)—Description and
travel. I. Title.
    PQ2247.P38 2006
    843'.8--dc22
    [B]

                                         2006031261

To Chris, Sam, and Tommy,
fellow Normandy explorers

Contents

Acknowledgments

In September, 2003, I convinced my husband that it would be a good idea to rent a cottage in Normandy. Never mind that said cottage was small, drafty, and inhabited by a large colony of mice. We were living at the time in a busy neighborhood of Paris, and in the months that followed, we would regularly pile our family of four into a rented Renault on Friday evenings and head west out of the city. Normandy's hilly apple orchards, historic villages, and vast sandy beaches soon made up for the dampness and scurrying rodents.

During our Normandy jaunts, we enjoyed a diverse array of tastes and experiences that kept us coming back. We scoured the markets for the freshest eggs and cheeses, made friends with a calvados producer, witnessed the birth of a lamb or two, and once faced down a charge by a group of ornery cows. In addition to enjoying the local color, I was fascinated with the literary associations of our new weekend getaway. Our cottage, or so reported our landlord, had figured in a novella by the author André Gide. And I remembered that the beach towns just twenty minutes away had also been important to Gustave Flaubert. As we wound our way toward the port town of Honfleur one day, I recalled the scene from his story "A Simple Heart," in which a maid named Félicité travels there on foot with her beloved pet parrot.

Even though the Normans are often reputed to be cool and distant, there are always exceptions to these stereotypes. When I returned to the area to research Flaubert's life in Normandy, I was welcomed and assisted by scholars, curators, and archivists as well as amateur "Flaubertistes." In particular, I would like to thank Daniel Fauvel of the Friends of Flaubert and de Maupassant in Rouen and Yvan Leclerc, professor at the University of Rouen, director of the Flaubert Center, and the brains behind an excellent website devoted to Flaubert (www.univ-rouen.fr/Flaubert), both of whom offered their time and insights during my stay. Arlette Dubois, curator at the Flaubert Museum in Rouen, also provided guidance and an impromptu tour of her collection. Joël Dupressoir, director of the town of Canteleu's multimedia library, showed me

Flaubert's library and sent me hard-to-find maps many months later. The staff of the Bibliothèque de Rouen, including Françoise Legendre and Thierry Ascencio-Parvy, guided me through the stacks of their library's impressive collection of Flaubert manuscripts and documents. I would also like to thank staff members in the tourism offices of Rouen, Trouville, and Ry.

My extended family deserves many thanks for putting up with me while I worked on this book. The largest share of my gratitude goes to my husband, Chris, first reader and greatest supporter, and my sons, Sam and Tommy, who discovered Normandy with me. My sister Sarah suggested that her husband, Peter Feichtmeir, join me on a trip to Normandy and he appeared one morning in Rouen, camera in hand. Many thanks to Peter for taking orders with good humor and producing many of the fine photographs that illustrate this book. Back in the Bay Area, my sister Mary let me use her basement as a work space and invited me to share in her delicious meals that sustained me during some long nights. Her husband, Roger Phelps, an amateur Flaubert scholar himself, offered constant encouragement as well as numerous books from his library. I would also like to thank my father-in-law, Norrell Noble, who braved the archives in the Bibliothèque Nationale in Paris in search of a photo, and my mother-in-law, Françoise Noble, who made sure my letters to French Flaubert experts were grammatically correct.

To my parents, Rosemary and Gray Patton, I offer my heartfelt thanks. Over the years, they have shared with me many memorable trips to France and encouraged my interest in a country half a world away. They also deserve credit for sleeping without a complaint in what may have been the world's most uncomfortable guest bed, located by chance in our Normandy cottage. My grandmothers, short-story writer and novelist Frances Gray Patton, and Ruth Coleman Dundas, world traveler and lifelong student, both inspired me to write from an early age.

Until recently, however, I have had a hard time finding the right book editors. For their encouragement and expert guidance, I thank Deirdre Greene and Nigel Quinney, who agreed that a book about a cantankerous writer from a damp region of France would not be entirely without interest.

A Journey into
Flaubert's
Normandy

Chapter 1
Gustave Flaubert
Normandy's Novelist

Flaubert refused for many years to have his picture taken or his portrait painted, but he yielded as he approached middle age.

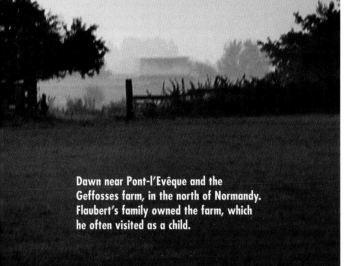

Dawn near Pont-l'Evêque and the Geffosses farm, in the north of Normandy. Flaubert's family owned the farm, which he often visited as a child.

Be regular and orderly in your life so that you may be violent and original in your work.

— Gustave Flaubert

On September 19, 1851, Gustave Flaubert started what many consider to be his masterpiece: *Madame Bovary*. Ensconced in his family home on the banks of the Seine, just outside of the city of Rouen in the French region of Normandy, he worked on the manuscript for the next four and a half years, laboring in isolation to write and rewrite what would become one of the first modern novels.

Flaubert had just returned from a two-year voyage to the Middle East and southern Europe with a close friend, Maxime Du Camp—the longest and farthest he ever ventured from his native Normandy—and he was initially unsure what he would write next. But even after this exotic journey, which he hoped would influence his work, he found the subject for his novel in the small-town Normandy that he knew intimately.

While he had been away, the local community had been scandalized by the tale of a doctor's wife, Delphine Delamare, who—so the story goes—poisoned herself at the age of twenty-seven after boredom with small-town life and her husband's mediocrity drove her to adultery and extravagant spending that led to debt. Her husband, who had been blind to her behavior, soon died as well, leaving behind their young daughter in the small Normandy town of Ry. Louis Bouilhet, a close friend and literary confidant, urged Flaubert to turn this drama into a novel.

Flaubert later declared that *Madame Bovary* was pure fabrication. Its setting, however—rural Normandy,

The west façade of the Cathédrale Notre-Dame, which dominates the center of Rouen. Much of the cathedral was built in the Norman gothic style in the thirteenth century.

revealed a love-hate relationship with the traditional and sometimes stifling mores of his slice of provincial northern France.

Growing up in Rouen, the onetime capital of Normandy, the writer developed a scorn for all that was "bourgeois," a term that for him referred less to social class and more to a close-minded, bigoted view of the world. For him, Rouen represented bourgeois society in its purest form. "Oh how I'd rather live in Spain, Italy, or even Provençe," he wrote to a boyhood friend, Ernest Chevalier, upon returning to Rouen from a trip to the south of France in 1840.

Throughout his life, however, Flaubert was faithful to Normandy. He was born and died there, and apart from occasional trips to the exotic Orient and jaunts to Paris, he rarely left the verdant region. While he criticized the repressive bourgeois attitudes, he also took inspiration from the beauty of this region's pastoral rolling hills, apple orchards, and seascapes.

Flaubert's Normandy, which cuts a swath from Rouen westward and northward through the Calvados region into countryside known as the Pays d'Auge, and northward to the Pays de Caux and the Côte Fleurie (Flower Coast), is filled with well-known sites such as Rouen's famous cathedral and the fabled Trouville beach. But it is also home to out-of-the-way villages, tightly knit farming communities, and hidden valleys. It is a region known for apple *cidre*, Calvados brandy, and aromatic Normandy cheeses, which small farmers still labor to produce. Indeed, two weeks before his death, Flaubert told his niece Caroline, "Sometimes I think I'm liquefying like an old Camembert."

with its farms and small towns—was real, and one with which he was well acquainted.

After the novel was published, Flaubert was charged with obscenity and brought to trial. He was later acquitted, but many Normans were horrified by his description of marital infidelity and hypocrisy in their region. In *Madame Bovary* and his other works, Flaubert

In addition to cheese, Normandy is known for its dampness, but travelers in this sometimes dreary climate are rewarded with the brilliant green of the hills and explosions of spring wildflowers. Storms move quickly across the English Channel, bringing heavy downpours that alternate with bright sunshine in the space of an afternoon. Flaubert recognized that the wet climate had an effect on the psyche, as he worked on his books in his family's damp house on the banks of the Seine. "If my book is any good it will tickle many a feminine wound," he wrote just after *Madame Bovary* was published. "One or two will smile when they recognize themselves. I will have known your sufferings, poor obscure souls, damp from your stifled sorrow, like your provincial backyards, where the moss grows on the walls."

The "Novelist's Novelist"

Flaubert was not a prolific writer, publishing only four novels, three short stories, and one play in his career.

Small farms dot the countryside near Ry.

Although he achieved some renown during his lifetime, he was recognized as great and influential only after his death in 1880. Since then, Normandy has claimed him as its most famous literary figure. Visitors to the area can track down his various homes, some of which are now museums, and trace his path through the small towns, farms, and coastline.

Flaubert's influence, however, has spread far beyond his native province and his country. Henry James called Flaubert "the novelist's novelist," and writers from Marcel Proust to Mario Vargas Llosa have acknowledged their indebtedness to his literary style. These writers took inspiration from Flaubert's continual search for *le mot juste* (the precise word) and his detailed observation of everyday life.

Unlike his predecessors, Flaubert declined to judge his characters and sought to remove the author from the narrative, leaving the reader to make up his or her own mind about the morality of his stories. In portraying scenes of daily life in small Norman towns and beyond, he sought to tell the truth, even if the harsh, realistic scenes were disturbing.

Although he is credited with laying the groundwork for the modern novel, Flaubert's work also reflects his love of history and of the classics. Shakespeare and Cervantes were his literary heroes, and as a young man he devoured the works of Romantic writers, including Johann Wolfgang von Goethe, Lord Byron, and Victor Hugo.

In 1842, however, at the age of twenty, Flaubert submitted to the wishes of his father, the chief surgeon at Rouen's city hospital, and began professional studies at law school in Paris. But he showed no interest in and little aptitude for the law, and in 1844 his studies were cut short by a health crisis that would change the course of his life. While driving a two-wheeled cabriolet with his brother along a dark country road near Pont-l'Evêque on a January evening, Flaubert felt "a torrent of flames . . . sudden as lightning . . . an instantaneous interruption of memory." It seemed as if, he later wrote, "everything in your head is going off at once like a thousand fireworks." He lost consciousness and fell to the floor of the carriage. It was his first attack of epilepsy.

Seeking calm for Gustave, the family soon moved to Croisset, and Dr. Flaubert conceded that a life of law would be too demanding for his suddenly fragile son. Gustave was delighted to finally have an excuse to live the quiet life of a writer that he craved. "My illness has brought one benefit, in that I am allowed to spend my time as I would like, a great thing in life," he wrote to a school friend in January 1845.

Flaubert would, from then on, have a hard time leaving his riverside Norman home. In letters to his close friends and his lover during an eight-year period, Flaubert voiced disgust with his native region and promised on several occasions to move to Paris, although he never did. "Why have I stayed in this

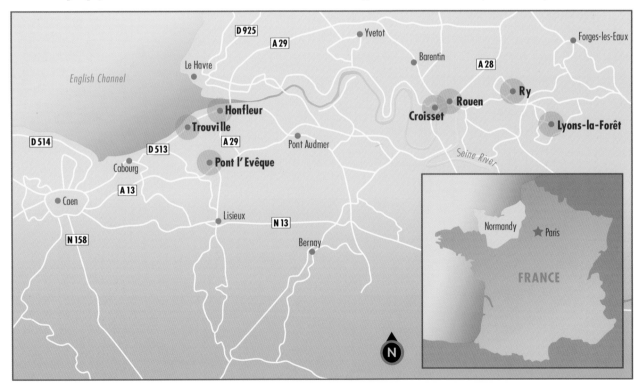

provincial backwater?" he asked his close friend Du Camp in 1851. "Must one not follow one's own path?" He was also an avid traveler who took great pleasure in his trips to Corsica, Italy, and the Middle East, and even treks around less distant regions such as Brittany and the south of France. In the end, however, it was a life of relative seclusion—broken by visits from members of his close literary circle and the companionship of his mother and his motherless niece, Caroline—that suited him best. "I live alone like a bear," he declared in 1845.

Alone in his study, writing into the early hours of the morning, Flaubert set to work to create his great novels. Along with Stendhal, who published *The Red and the Black* in 1830, and Honoré de Balzac, who wrote a series of novels under the title *The Human Comedy*, Flaubert is considered to be one of the creators of literary realism. Emile Zola, his friend and protégé, carried on the tradition. Flaubert rejected membership in any school, however, saying that he strove only to achieve "beauty," and his novels sometimes oscillate between realism and romanticism.

The beach at Trouville.

Flaubert's Landscape

Flaubert spent most of his working life at his family's manor just outside of Rouen, but he felt equally at home on the beaches of Trouville, the farmland surrounding Pont-l'Evêque, the chalky plateau northwest of Rouen, or retracing the narrow streets of his native city.

A journey through the landscape that shaped Flaubert's life and work begins in his birthplace, the port city of Rouen, an ancient city made prosperous over the centuries by the free flow of trade along the Seine from the English Channel to Paris. The city was also hit hard over the years by the plague and other contagious maladies imported along with valuable goods. To take care of the hordes of sick citizens, the city built a large religious hospital, the Hôtel Dieu, near the great cathedral.

Flaubert and his two siblings, Achille and Caroline, spent their earliest years living in a wing of this hospital (which had by then moved across town), where their father practiced surgery. Dr. Flaubert's dissection room looked out on the family's garden, and Gustave and his sister would climb a trellis to view the corpses. Images from the hospital and from his father's practice emerge frequently in Flaubert's work, most notably in *Madame Bovary*, in which he describes the professional life and misfortunes of a country doctor in detail.

This small pavilion in Croisset is all that remains of the Flaubert family's property.

his Parisian friends to join him. Painters Corot, Boudin, Monet, and Pissarro later came to paint its seascapes and cliffs. The ancient oyster-fishing village gradually took on glamour as the nineteenth century progressed, especially after train service from Paris began.

In April 1844, Flaubert's father bought an eighteenth-century house at Croisset, just a few miles downstream from Rouen along the Seine. Flaubert was recovering from his first attack of epilepsy and had abandoned his law studies in Paris. From 1851 to his death in 1880, his life and the inspiration for much of his work would revolve around his close relatives in the region and the house at Croisset.

Although much of Croisset was later destroyed to build a factory, visitors come regularly to view the pavilion that remains and to stroll along the Seine near where Flaubert spent much of his life. The pavilion now houses a small Flaubert museum, which looks lost amid the modern and industrial development that has transformed the village over the past century.

Flaubert never lived in the town of Ry, but this quiet country town—just fifteen minutes south of the busy center of Rouen—considers itself the real-life Yonville-l'Abbaye, the fictional town that is the setting for *Madame Bovary*. In fact, the Bovary connection has become the town's main industry, with the supposed homes of the Delamares/Bovarys preserved as museums, and a Bovary Gallery complete with dramatizations of

In July 1836, just before his fifteenth birthday, Flaubert vacationed with his family in the resort town of Trouville, a fishing village on the Normandy coast that was becoming increasingly popular with Parisians for its long, wide, sandy beaches and dramatic cliff walks. A chance meeting that summer on a Trouville beach with a married, older woman sparked Flaubert's first great love—albeit unrequited—and served as the inspiration for Madame Arnoux, the central character in his novel *Sentimental Education.*

Trouville, which sits across the river from its sister city, Deauville, got its start as a literary and artistic destination in the early nineteenth century, when writer Alexander Dumas came to stay and encouraged

famous scenes from the novel. In 1990, 140 years after the town first laid her to rest under a cloud of gossip and disgrace, the local literary society and chamber of commerce paid for a new tombstone for Delamare's grave, which lies just outside the town church.

This journey through Flaubert's landscape ends, paradoxically, with a place he knew well as a child. From his early years, Flaubert spent holidays with his family just outside Pont-l'Evêque, a quintessential Norman town not far from the Deauville and Trouville beaches. His story of a small-town maid and her parrot, "A Simple Heart," is set in this historic capital of the

Pays d'Auge, surrounded by green hills and dairy farms. This fertile corner of Normandy is perhaps best known for its cheese, first made in Roman times. Flaubert knew the town and region well from his childhood visits; "A Simple Heart" is clearly autobiographical, and is full of nostalgia and affection for Pont-l'Evêque and its surroundings.

Family Ties

Flaubert's ties to Normandy began with his mother's family. While the Flauberts originally came from the Champagne region northeast of Normandy, his mother, Anne-Caroline Fleuriot, was descended from the Cambremers of Croixmare, a Normandy family.

During their early years in Rouen, the Flaubert family enjoyed good standing among the community and blissful summer vacations at a vacation house in Déville-lès-Rouen, on the vast beaches at Trouville, and then at the large white house at Croisset.

The period of happiness was short-lived. In 1846, Dr. Flaubert discovered a large abscess on his leg, likely the result of an accidental wound from his own scalpel. In an effort to save him, Flaubert's brother, Achille, operated and attempted to drain the wound. But in these days before the discovery of penicillin, the gangrene spread, and Dr. Flaubert died in January 1846 at the age of sixty-one. That same year Flaubert's sister, Caroline, gave birth to a baby girl, but never recovered from the childbirth and died two months later from puerperal fever. "It seems that calamity is upon us, and that it will not leave until it has

The Touques River runs alongside the Eglise Saint-Michel in Pont-l'Evêque, a church that plays a central role in Flaubert's story "A Simple Heart."

glutted itself on us," Flaubert wrote to Maxime Du Camp several days before his sister's death.

A Norman Identity

Despite his illness, Gustave did not appear the fragile invalid. He was tall, broad-shouldered, and blond with green eyes—traits reminiscent of the Viking invaders who had conquered the region in the tenth century, leaving their mark on the people and landscape. Flaubert protested to friends, however, that he didn't feel like a descendant of "savage" Vikings. Instead, he was enchanted with the cultures of the Mediterranean and the art and architecture of antiquity. "I hate Europe, France—my own country, my succulent motherland that I'd gladly send to hell now that I've had a glimpse of what lies beyond," he wrote to boyhood friend Ernest Chevalier in 1840, just after his first trip to Corsica. "I think I must have been transplanted by the winds to this land of mud; surely I was born elsewhere— I've always had what seem like memories or intuitions of perfumed shores and blue seas."

If Flaubert railed against his fellow Normans and Rouennais, he was also one of them. He traveled far, and set his writings in exotic locales at times, but he did the work from his desk in his study in his Norman house just up the Seine from his birthplace. When traveling through the outskirts of Cairo with Du Camp, he wrote with nostalgia of his house at Croisset. Back home, his predictable—if eccentric at times—routine, in the countryside that he knew so well, suited him and helped him to concentrate on his work.

During the years he spent laboring over *Madame Bovary* in his study at Croisset, he wrote often to his longtime lover, Louise Colet, describing both the difficulties and the satisfaction he found in the process. "What a heavy oar the pen is, and what a strong current ideas are to row in! This makes me so desperate that I enjoy it considerably. In this state I spent a good day today, with the window open, the sun on the river, and the greatest serenity in the world."

These moments of joy were interspersed with long periods of gloom. "It is strange how I was born with little faith in happiness," he wrote in 1846, and then declared in a letter to Du Camp, "I hate life." Flaubert

Cows graze amid the apple trees in the Calvados region.

made it through his fits of depression with the help of close male friends, including fellow Norman writers Louis Bouilhet, Alfred Le Poittevin, and, later, Le Poittevin's nephew, Guy de Maupassant. With these companions he spent many hours reading his work, talking, smoking, and philosophizing. He also ventured out with them to Paris and beyond.

Flaubert's mother, Anne-Caroline Fleuriot, was born in Pont-l'Evêque and descended from a long line of Normans. She was thirty-eight-years old in this portrait, in which she wears an intricate hair knot fashionable at the time.

In February 1848, he traveled with Bouilhet and Du Camp to Paris to observe the "beautiful revolution," an insurrection of workers and enlightened bourgeois against the aristocracy. Without much bloodshed, the uprising toppled the corrupt regime of King Louis-Philippe, putting in place the Second Empire. This period of giddy political reform was short-lived, however. In 1851, Louis Napoléon Bonaparte, known as "the people's prince," was elected president of France. He quickly became a tyrant, however, and Flaubert was later to suffer from the repressive attitude and censorship of the regime.

An Observer of History

Flaubert stayed largely on the sidelines of his century's turbulent rebellions and political changes. He loved art and literature above all and repudiated all political parties, left and right. He expressed his views in a letter to the writer George Sand, with whom he developed a close friendship later in his life. Whereas Sand advocated universal suffrage, Flaubert declared that he was worth twenty other Croisset voters, and said he would prefer a government by a mandarinate. Sand saw the proletariat in a positive way, but Flaubert distrusted the masses and said he would grant them "liberty but not power." He also mocked the scientific and industrial progress of his century, calling industry "stupid" and showing little faith that such advances would improve the human condition.

Flaubert's pessimistic view of mankind intensified after the Prussians conquered France in 1870. At one point he was forced

11

out of his house at Croisset when a group of Prussian soldiers took up residence for a brief period. "Perhaps race wars are going to begin again?" Flaubert wrote to Sand prophetically. "Over the next hundred years we shall see several million men killing each other at a single sitting. All of the Orient against all of Europe, the old world against the new."

Mama's Boy

Although often criticized for his harsh view of the world, Flaubert also showed signs of compassion. He helped raise and educate his motherless niece, Caroline, and wept at the deaths of close friends. After *Madame Bovary* was published, he responded to a letter from a fifty-six-year-old admirer of his work, Marie-Sophie Leroyer de Chantepie, and then, although he never met her, carried on a long, affectionate correspondence with the lonely woman.

Flaubert never married and spent most of his life living in the comfort of his family home with his mother, despite carrying on several love affairs. After she died, he wrote that "my poor dear Mother was the person I have loved most. It feels as though a piece of my guts has been torn out."

Flaubert stayed at Croisset for the remainder of his life, reciting his work to friends and, increasingly, to the trees and flowers outside his window. In his last years, as he lost his friends and family in increasing numbers, Flaubert surrounded himself with the familiar elements of his Normandy landscape: lush green meadows bursting with flowers, rows of lindens, and the Seine River, which winds its way though the fields and towns toward the sea.

A rusty bicycle and bright flowers adorn a side street in Lyons-la Forêt.

For Emma Bovary, Flaubert's doomed heroine, the provincial city of Rouen appears out the window of her carriage as a paradise filled with culture, excitement, and glamour, a sanctuary from the monotony and disappointment of her small-town life. "To her the old Norman city was like some fabulous capital, a Babylon into which she was making her entry." The monuments, streets, and squares of Rouen play a central role in Flaubert's classic novel, and the writer describes them almost as vividly as the characters themselves.

As he prepared to write *Madame Bovary*, Flaubert traveled down the river from his country home to his birthplace to find his childhood landmarks, record their details, and incorporate them into his fiction. The writer did not share his celebrated character's enthusiasm for his native city, however. In September 1843, at the age of twenty-two, for example, he wrote to his childhood friend Ernest Chevalier to complain about the provincial town. He admired Rouen for its history and the many important writers born there, but he lashed out at its middle-class, snobbish residents. Rouen has "beautiful churches and stupid inhabitants," he wrote.

Throughout his life, Flaubert expressed disdain for Rouen and its people. In letters to friends and in his *Dictionary of Accepted Ideas*, he catalogued what he considered "the stupidities" of the growing class of comfortably well-off and educated people that populated his hometown. Its damp climate and

Then, all at once, the city came into view. Sloping downward like an amphitheater, drowned in mist, it sprawled out shapelessly beyond its bridges. Then open fields swept upward again in a monotonous curve, merging at the top with the uncertain line of the pale sky. Thus seen from above, the whole landscape had the static quality of a painting: ships at anchor were crowded into one corner, the river traced its curve along the foot of the green hills, and on the water the oblong-shaped islands looked like great black fish stopped in their course. . . . A kind of intoxication was wafted up to her from those closely packed lives, and her heart swelled as though the 120,000 souls palpitating below had sent up to her as a collective offering the breath of all the passions she supposed them to be feeling.

—Flaubert, *Madame Bovary*

provincial attitudes clashed with the Romanticism in vogue at the time, which glorified the passion and warmth associated with Mediterranean and Middle Eastern countries.

At the same time, Flaubert had a firm attachment to the city. He spent most of his early life there and then returned regularly to see friends, show off the churches and monuments to out-of-town visitors, and seek inspiration for his work. No other place had a greater influence on his writing than Rouen, although he cultivated his role as an outsider to Rouen society until his death.

In return, nineteenth-century Rouen largely disapproved of Flaubert and his work, if it knew anything about the writer at all. Émile Zola, the great realistic novelist and contemporary of Flaubert's,

described the small funeral procession for the writer that wound its way through the city and up to the cemetery, concluding that, at the time of his death, Flaubert was unknown by most in Rouen. His small white tombstone, next to the larger grey stones of his parents and surrounded by the city's "bourgeois" that he loved to criticize, now looks down on the city, which reevaluated him after his death and came to cherish him as a favorite son.

In Rouen today, reminders of the writer are everywhere. Flaubert's statue presides over the Place des Carmes, a leafy square filled with café tables and flocks of schoolchildren. Plaques point out the residences of his families and friends, and the family's apartment at the Hôtel Dieu, the city hospital where his father was chief surgeon, is now the Musée Flaubert, a museum dedicated to Flaubert's life, his family, and the history of medicine.

Flaubert's characters and stories also live on in modern-day Rouen. In *Madame Bovary*, Emma meets her lover, Léon, at ❶ **the Cathédrale Notre-Dame,** on the **Place de la Cathédrale,** where an annoyingly thorough Swiss guide delays their tryst with his lengthy tour of the church. Finally, Léon sweeps Emma away into a closed carriage and takes her on a rollicking trip around Rouen, a scene that shocked readers at the time and contributed to Flaubert's prosecution, just after the book was published, for offending public morals.

Back inside the cathedral, a stained glass window depicting the legend of Saint Julian, or Julian the Poor, inspired Flaubert to write a short story interpreting the life of this hunter who is cursed to kill his parents and finally becomes a beggar before taking pity on a leper and rising to heaven.

Some settings have obviously changed considerably over the past two centuries. ❷ **The Théâtre des Arts, 7 rue du Dr. Rambert,** where the stumbling country doctor Charles Bovary brings his unhappy wife to distract her, burned down in 1872, was rebuilt, and was then destroyed again during World War II. In 1962, the city built a new theater in its place along the banks of the Seine. The newer theater's concrete, modern design contrasts with the old city's medieval and Renaissance feel.

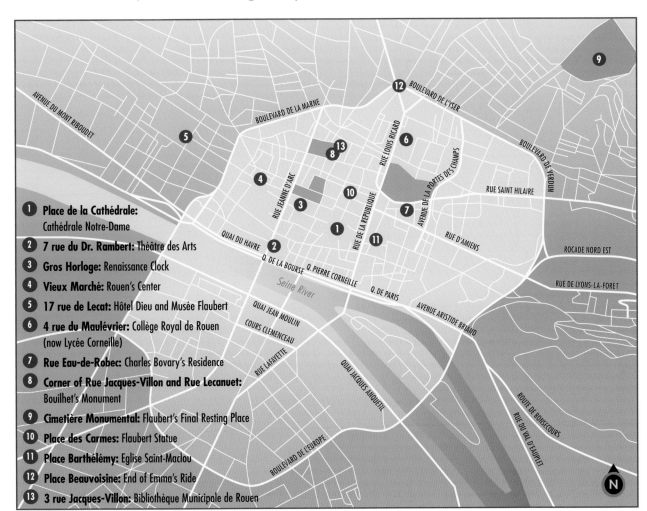

❶ **Place de la Cathédrale:** Cathédrale Notre-Dame

❷ **7 rue du Dr. Rambert:** Théâtre des Arts

❸ **Gros Horloge:** Renaissance Clock

❹ **Vieux Marché:** Rouen's Center

❺ **17 rue de Lecat:** Hôtel Dieu and Musée Flaubert

❻ **4 rue du Maulévrier:** Collège Royal de Rouen (now Lycée Corneille)

❼ **Rue Eau-de-Robec:** Charles Bovary's Residence

❽ **Corner of Rue Jacques-Villon and Rue Lecanuet:** Bouilhet's Monument

❾ **Cimetière Monumental:** Flaubert's Final Resting Place

❿ **Place des Carmes:** Flaubert Statue

⓫ **Place Barthélémy:** Eglise Saint-Maclou

⓬ **Place Beauvoisine:** End of Emma's Ride

⓭ **3 rue Jacques-Villon:** Bibliothèque Municipale de Rouen

Rouen Today

The ancient capital of Normandy and the region's largest city, with a population of 380,000, Rouen sits on a wide bend in the Seine roughly fifty-five miles from its mouth at the English Channel and functions as the port of Paris. The city is far from a tourist mecca, but it boasts a rich history, much of it well preserved in its old central district despite devastating bombing raids by Allied forces at the end of World War II. Those bombardments, which damaged the famed cathedral and leveled part of the city, were only the most recent in a long line of attacks over the centuries.

Rouen, now a thriving industrial port and cultural center of Normandy, is a survivor that has continually bounced back. The central district is packed with students well into the evening, and the flower-rimmed promenade along the river hums with children's bicycles and families pushing strollers. Tour groups congregate in the medieval central district and in front of the cathedral.

Parts of the city have been destroyed over the centuries, however, and have been transformed even since Flaubert's time. Large cranes that load freight on and off ships line the river just outside the city, and the industrial zone is plainly visible from a bridge in the city's center. Modern apartment buildings and offices have replaced entire neighborhoods wiped out in the 1944 bombings, and the bohemian neighborhood where Emma Bovary wanders alone after attending a masked ball no longer exists.

Still, in the narrow pedestrian streets of the old town, much remains unchanged, including sixteenth-century half-timbered houses crisscrossed with wooden struts across plastered brick façades. Gothic churches and famous monuments such as ❸ the Gros Horloge

(literally, "large clock")—a Renaissance pavilion set on an arch with an embellished clock—still dot the city's skyline. The intricate façade of Rouen's cathedral, made famous by a series of paintings by Monet, rises in the city's center, and its various towers and steeples tell Rouen's history from the twelfth century to the present. Construction of the rib-vaulted cathedral started

The half-timbered architecture and cobblestone streets of old Rouen evoke medieval times, when people, animals, and vehicles crowded through the narrow, dark passages.

around A.D. 1144, with each century adding its touch until a cast-iron spire replaced a wooden one destroyed in an 1822 fire. (Flaubert hated industry and "progress" and vehemently opposed the iron spire's addition at the time.) More recently, a pinnacle fell through the roof during a severe storm in December 1999, and the cathedral is in a continuous state of repair.

The Renaissance clock known as the Gros Horloge was moved to its current location in 1527 from its former home in Rouen's belfry. The clock's single hand tells the hour, while its central section indicates the phases of the moon. The arch's underside is decorated with carvings depicting the Good Shepherd and his flock.

Rouen's famous literary figures are also on full display in the center of town. Pierre Corneille, the seventeenth-century playwright known for *Le Cid* and much admired by Flaubert, was born in 1606 in Rouen; his house is now a museum dedicated to his life and work. Corneille, for Flaubert, signified the artistic greatness to which he aspired. When Flaubert's lover, Louise Colet, proclaimed one day that she wouldn't exchange her happiness with Flaubert "for the fame of Corneille," he was appalled. "What is fame!" he proclaimed angrily to Colet in a letter of November 7, 1847. "It is nothing. A mere noise, the external accompaniment of the joy Art gives us. 'The fame of Corneille' indeed! But—to be Corneille! To feel one's self Corneille!" Corneille studied at a Jesuit school, the Collège Royal de Rouen (now called the Lycée Corneille), whose well-known graduates include Flaubert himself, as well as his younger disciple, Guy de Maupassant.

A Tumultuous History

Rouen was founded in pre-Roman times, but it got its name when Julius Caesar defeated the resident Celts in 56 B.C. and the Romans turned the city into their regional capital, naming it Rotomagus, a derivation of the Celtic name Ratuma, hence Rouen. The Romans and Germanic tribes coexisted in Normandy for several centuries. In Rouen, Christianity took hold some fifty years before the emperor Constantine made the religion official. Rouen's first bishop, the Welsh missionary Saint Mellon, was named in A.D. 260.

Monet's Cathedral

In February 1892, Claude Monet set up his easel in a room opposite Rouen's Cathédrale Notre-Dame and started painting. From his perch in a rented apartment, the artist produced more than thirty oil paintings of the Gothic façade over a period of two years. During this time, he often kept peculiar hours, rising before dawn and retiring just after twilight, to capture the transient effects of light and atmosphere on the great church. The result was the series, painted at different times, in different weather conditions, famous today for the delicate show of light, color, and atmosphere that helped to define the Impressionist period.

Monet occupied more than one room during this period so as to capture the cathedral from slightly different angles. At one point, he painted from a room in a building that originally housed the city's ministry of finance. Now that room is a part of Rouen's tourist office, and journalists, art historians, and camera crews rotate in and out of Monet's former painting lair. Outside, crowds of tourists and residents stroll through the massive stone square in front of the cathedral to gaze at the intricate towers that soar upward from its twelfth-century foundation. For centuries the cathedral has served as the center of town, and it remains Rouen's most important monument. The city now uses the cathedral's façade for a dramatic nighttime light show meant to bring Monet's technique to the digital age, although some traditionalists abhor the spectacle.

"Everything changes. Even stone," Monet wrote in a letter. His series of paintings of Rouen's Cathédrale Notre-Dame depicts the effects of changing light on the monument's intricate Gothic façade.

This map of Rouen was published in 1572.

Norsemen raided the city repeatedly in the ninth century, and by the tenth century Rouen was the capital of Normandy. Rollo, the chief of the plundering Vikings, shook hands with Charles the Simple of France in 911, creating the new duchy of Normandy. Rollo promptly changed his name to Robert and married the king's daughter. Thus began three centuries of rule by Norman dukes with Rouen as their home base, provoking a lengthy and bitter struggle with England. The English held the city from 1419 to 1449 in the Hundred Years' War, and Joan of Arc, perhaps its most famous resident, was tried and burned at the stake there in 1431.

Joan of Arc, or Jeanne d'Arc, was not born in Normandy. She was the daughter of a farmer from the border area of the Champagne and Lorraine regions. As a young girl, she started to hear "voices" of saints, and by the time she was a teenager these voices were urging her to go help the dauphin—later to be named King Charles VII—who was being kept from the throne by the English. Dressed as a man, Joan led French troops to victory over the English at Orléans. In 1430 she was captured, sold to the English, and turned over to the eccle-siastical court at Rouen. She was tried for heresy and witchcraft before French clerics who supported the English, and was put to death after first recanting and then, shortly afterward, proclaiming her innocence.

Joan's martyrdom in Rouen's ❹ **Vieux Marché** (old market), now a bustling square lined with restaurants and cafés, marked a symbolic turning point in the war with England. The execution coincided with the duke of Burgundy's switch of allegiance from England to France; thereafter, England was in retreat from forays into France. English troops left Paris in 1436, and although fortresses such as the port of Honfleur continued to change hands for years, by 1450 England had lost its last stronghold in Normandy.

Rouen commemorates its martyr in numerous ways. Streets are named after her; a memorial at the old market is dedicated to her; even the chocolate-covered almonds popular in the city are known as "Joan of Arc's tears." Joan was tried and later threatened with torture in what is now called the Joan of Arc Tower, part of a castle built by King Philippe Auguste in 1204. Executions still occurred

Pierre Corneille studied law but went on to become one of the greatest French dramatists of the seventeenth century, along with Molière and Racine.

in the Vieux Marché during Flaubert's time; he recalled walking through the square and seeing blood on the stones from a recent guillotining.

Despite its sometimes tragic and violent history, Rouen benefited over the centuries from its prime location on the Seine between Paris and the English Channel. "One of the most beautiful trade routes ever formed by nature," wrote the ancient Greek geographer Strabo. The city was built at a section of the river where the ocean tides lose their strength; it was, until the mid-twentieth century, the last place before the sea where bridges could be built.

Though prosperous, Rouen also endured an array of imported diseases over the centuries. With its tangle of narrow streets filled with animals and streams of raw sewage, the city was ravaged by the plague in the Middle Ages. When it was theorized that the illness was spread "through the air," the city forbade any further construction of the inward-leaning rooftops that left little room between the houses, although some remnants of this type of architecture remain in the streets just behind the cathedral.

A Doctor Comes to Town

Achille-Cléophas Flaubert, the son of a veterinarian from the Champagne region of northern France, aimed to become more than just a country doctor. He studied medicine at the Hôtel Dieu in Paris with a celebrated surgeon, Guillaume Dupuytren, and received top prizes for his diligence and academic excellence. Flaubert's biographers theorize that Dupuytren arranged for his star pupil to take a job at Rouen's great public hospital, several days' journey from Paris, out of professional jealousy. But Dupuytren might also have helped Dr. Flaubert avoid the draft during these times of

Napoleonic battles by obtaining a medical certificate for him stating that the young doctor had symptoms of tuberculosis.

Achille-Cléophas arrived in Rouen in November 1806, twenty-two years old, single, and determined to succeed. His medical certificate described him as "five feet nine inches tall, with brown eyes, an oval-shaped face, a long nose and a small chin." His new city, although a step down from Paris, was one of France's largest urban centers. In 1800, Rouen was the fifth-largest city in France, with a population of around 85,000. It was a commercial and industrial city above all, an important textile-manufacturing center. British writers who traveled in Normandy in the late eighteenth century called Rouen "the Manchester of France," and one such scribe, Arthur Young, described it as "this great, ugly, stinking, close and ill-built town, which is full of nothing but dirt and industry."

Politically, Rouen suffered less from the upheaval of the French Revolution than did other cities in Normandy. In contrast to its bloody past, there were only nine executions in the town, even during the worst of the Reign of Terror that swept through France in the years following the storming of the Bastille in 1789. Wealthy merchants and manufacturers had welcomed the fall of France's royalty, but they favored a more moderate and liberal revolution that respected order—and their property. When Dr. Flaubert arrived in Rouen, Napoléon had been emperor for two years, and the city, as well as the rest of France, was caught up in a patriotic mood. The feeling of the time is captured in a local newspaper announcement at the time for *The Dream*, a Christmas spectacle playing at Rouen's Théâtre des Arts:

> *The high deeds which continue to distinguish the genius of the emperor and the courage of his great*

Dr. Achille-Cléophas Flaubert, Gustave's father, came from the Champagne region of France. He arrived in Rouen in 1806 to begin an illustrious career as chief surgeon at the Hôtel Dieu.

and valiant army offer to the imagination such wonders that we are inclined to think we are dreaming when we read the bulletins which set out each glorious circumstance, were it not for the fact that we are in the century of marvels, quite accustomed to seeing ever new and ever more extraordinary things brought about.

Dr. Flaubert, never a soldier, was less impressed by the *gloire* of the Napoleonic era than were many fellow Rouennais. Instead, he devoted himself to his work of dissecting corpses and teaching anatomy, seeking glory in a more methodical way. As the doctor set out to

make a name for himself as a surgeon in Rouen, the city's merchants and notables were suffering from the effects of an embargo on trade with Britain, which cut shipping tonnage to pre-Revolution levels. Profound change in the textile industry, however, helped to keep the city prosperous. During the Napoleonic era, the city's booming textile trade moved from labor-intensive methods to more widespread use of mechanization, such as water-powered spinning mills.

While the industrial revolution made its mark on Rouen and political regimes transformed European society, Dr. Flaubert focused on his work. Although he was considered a liberal with anticlerical tendencies and was attached to the principles of the Revolution of 1789, he showed little interest in governments, as long as he could continue to study and practice surgery unimpeded.

At the Hôtel Dieu, Dr. Flaubert was apprenticed to Jean-Baptiste Laumonier, known for making gruesome-looking life-size wax models of the half-dissected human form. If the young doctor looked down on this practice, favoring actual dissection of human corpses, he recognized that Laumonier had influence and standing in the community. Laumonier also had a dark-haired niece named Anne-Caroline Fleuriot, an orphan who had come to live in the hospital as a teenager. Dr. Flaubert, after presenting his thesis on "the care of sick before and after surgical operations" in 1810, could have left Rouen for good. However, he stayed, and married Caroline in February 1812 at the Eglise de la Madeleine.

A Hospital for a Home

Soon after their marriage, the doctor and his new wife moved to an apartment on the Rue du Petit-Salut,

The Hôtel Dieu was once Rouen's main hospital but now serves as the regional government headquarters.

built its first hospital for plague victims outside city limits in the sixteenth century. In 1758, the city's sick were transferred to the new hospital on the other side of town. Rouen moved its hospital to the far eastern section of the city in the early 1990s, and the building now serves as the *préfecture*, or regional government headquarters.

The museum that remains, the Musée Flaubert, displays portraits of the Flaubert family and the surgeons who came before them, as well as items from Flaubert's life such as a stuffed parrot that, the museum's curator claims, is the one the writer borrowed from the city's natural history museum for inspiration while writing "A Simple Heart."

where their first son, Achille, was born. In 1818, Laumonier died and Achille-Cléophas took over as chief of surgery at ❺ **the Hôtel Dieu, 17 rue de Lecat,** giving the family the right to move into an apartment in the eastern wing of the grand hospital.

This three-story apartment, which looks out on a small garden on one side and a large courtyard on the other, was traditionally occupied by the hospital's chief of surgery, an important position that commanded respect throughout the city. The first occupant, Claude-Nicolas Le Cat, whose portrait adorns the wall on the ground floor, founded the Academy of Sciences, Humanities, and Arts in Rouen. The apartment is now a small museum devoted to Flaubert's life and to the history of medicine, an odd combination that reflects the fact that it still belongs to Rouen's hospital.

The large, stately hospital was constructed in the seventeenth and eighteenth centuries, well after Rouen

Gustave was born in 1821 in an alcove of his parents' bedroom on the apartment's second floor. The room is furnished in the bourgeois style of the time, with drapes and velvet, although there are few records that describe the setting. The Flaubert children slept on the third floor of the apartment in the massive hospital's eastern wing, where the Musée Flaubert now has its offices and plans to expand its exhibition of medical artifacts and Flaubert paraphernalia. The third-floor alcoves look out on the large courtyard and over the city's grey rooftops, church spires, and factory chimneys, a view that has changed little since Flaubert slept there as a child. Three stories down is the large courtyard, where sick patients sat under shade trees in the summer months.

The Parrot

The curator of Rouen's Musée Flaubert picks up the somewhat dusty stuffed green parrot and turns it over. "This is definitely the right parrot," she says. "Just look at the writing." Elsewhere, just outside of Rouen—at the Pavillon de Croisset, the stone garden pavilion that stands near the former site of the Flaubert family's riverside estate—another curator points to a stuffed green parrot, also claimed to be the bird that the writer borrowed from the city's Museum of Natural History in 1875. That parrot sat atop Flaubert's writing table while he composed "A Simple Heart," a short story written near the end of his life that chronicles the life of a simple and devout Pont-l'Evêque maid and her beloved parrot, Loulou.

"I'm writing with an 'Amazon' standing on my writing table, his beak askew, gazing at me with his glass eyes," Flaubert wrote to his niece, Caroline. "The sight of the thing is beginning to annoy me. But I'm keeping him there, to fill my mind with the idea of parrothood."

Which is the real parrot? The English writer Julian Barnes ponders this question in his novel *Flaubert's Parrot*, which tracks amateur Flaubert expert Geoffrey Braithwaite's jaunt through Flaubert country and examines his musings on the writer's life and his own. In the end Braithwaite finds that, in fact, neither of the two parrots is

Is this the right parrot?

likely genuine, and Flaubert's parrot could have been any one of the dozens once stored at Rouen's Museum of Natural History, which is now closed to the public.

"Why does the writing make us chase the writer?" Barnes's main character muses in the book's opening chapter. "Why can't we leave well enough alone? Why aren't the books enough? Flaubert wanted them to be: few writers believed more in the objectivity of the written text and the insignificance of the writer's personality; yet still we disobediently pursue."

No one knows which stuffed parrot actually sat on Flaubert's desk. The unanswered question still causes Flaubert scholars' eyes to sparkle. In 1859, the writer Ernest Feydeau wrote to Flaubert asking for biographical details. "I have no biography," Flaubert replied, and he complained:

As soon as you become an artist, it seems that grocers, legal registrars, customs clerks, bootboys, and others feel themselves obliged to take a personal interest in your life. And there are others to inform them whether you are dark or fair, witty or melancholic, how many summers you have lived, and whether you are a devotee of the bottle or keen on playing the mouth-organ. I, on the other hand, believe that a writer should leave behind him nothing but his works.

At the time of Flaubert's birth, Rouen was just recovering from the fall of the Napoleonic Empire and a return to rule by the Bourbons. Families of draftees and local merchants, longing for overseas trade, had applauded the Restoration, a striking change of course after the revolutionary and Napoleonic years. The Hôtel Dieu was just outside of the city's center, but the Flaubert family was only a few blocks away from Rouen's thriving port, as well as museums, a botanical garden, numerous churches, and medieval and Renaissance monuments. The city was also an intellectual and cultural center; its public library stored 32,000 books and 1,200 ancient manuscripts.

Dr. Flaubert, though engrossed in his medical practice and teaching, also participated in the city's intellectual elite as a member of the Académie des Sciences, Belle-Lettres et Arts de Rouen. Rouen society, made up largely of wealthy merchants and textile manufacturers, respected the doctor for his medical achievements and stature among the country's top doctors, even if his views were more liberal than some in this conservatively inclined city. In 1826, a Paris review called him "one of France's most important doctors."

Flaubert and his siblings also admired their father and spent their playtime watching him work. Even before he started school, Flaubert and his siblings peered in at dissections, observed the mentally ill, and examined human skulls. At the age of five or six, he later told the writer George Sand in a letter that he had wanted to "send my heart to a little girl I was in love with (I mean my actual heart). I could see it on a bed of straw, in a hamper, a hamper full of oysters."

Today the Musée Flaubert's exhibits include a wide range of medical curiosities, including a collection of phrenological heads: plaster casts of famous men, meant to illustrate a pseudoscience invented by a doctor named F. J. Galli in the late eighteenth century. According to the theory, phrenology—the analysis of bumps on a person's skull—could reveal that person's moral and intellectual abilities. Flaubert wrote about phrenology in *Madame Bovary*.

Much of the museum's other medical paraphernalia reflects themes and images from Flaubert's writing as well. In a ground-floor room that served as Dr. Flaubert's consultation room, for example, a large book describes surgical methods for treating clubfoot. Flaubert borrowed the book from his doctor brother while writing the section of *Madame Bovary* in which Charles Bovary attempts the operation, with disastrous results.

The museum also documents the state of medicine at the time and reflects Dr. Flaubert's stature as an early practitioner of surgeries to remove tumors and correct birth defects. In the days before anesthesia and antibiotics, patients died at a high rate from complications during and after the operations. Dr. Flaubert worked intently to find the best techniques in preoperative and postoperative care.

Flaubert at the age of nine.

Rouen Adopts a Family

Although their three children were born in the city, neither Flaubert's father nor mother were natives. Flaubert's mother, Anne-Caroline Fleuriot, was a Norman from Pont-l'Evêque, a city surrounded by lush farmland west of Rouen, known for its cheese and Calvados, an apple brandy. Flaubert was close to his mother and lived with her for most of his life; his nostalgia for the Pays d'Auge, which he used as the setting for his story "A Simple Heart," stems from childhood trips to visit his mother's family in the area.

Achille Flaubert, Gustave's brother, in a drawing dated 1836.

the patient a glass of wine, and narcotics such as opium or camphor could be administered to help the patient sleep. Above all, the doctor must remain calm at all times.

Dr. Flaubert had aimed higher than his own father, and had worked hard to become Rouen's leading surgeon. Madame Flaubert had been living at the Hôtel Dieu and also appreciated the rigor necessary to run the hospital. The Flauberts formed a tight partnership: Dr. Flaubert devoted himself to the hospital and later to building a fortune by buying property in the Normandy countryside; Madame Flaubert oversaw their children's education and managed the family's growing wealth. Flaubert's older brother, Achille, took on the responsibility of following in his father's footsteps, while Gustave and his younger sister, Caroline, were free to roam in the garden outside their hospital apartment.

Rouen society quickly accepted Dr. Flaubert as one of its own, and the family fit in well in this city that valued tradition and heritage. Dr. Flaubert was hardworking, disciplined, and an early advocate of "scientific medicine." However, while he believed that doctors should focus on the scientific side of their practice, he also urged that they not lose sight of the importance of human feelings. According to his thesis, surgeons needed to be attentive to their patients' mental state and should try to reassure them before an operation. Patients should never be allowed to see the surgical instruments before the operation, and they should be allowed to scream during an operation as a means to alleviate pain. Anxiety and fear should be reduced by all means possible to cut the risk of infection. After the operation, the doctor should offer

Flaubert describes his early childhood in largely idyllic terms, listing his favorite occupations as "reading, reverie, poetry, the theater." His father worked nearby, he was close to his mother and his sister, and his nanny doted on him and helped him to learn his letters. Béatrix Caroline Hébert, born in the nearby Eure district, came to work for the Flauberts in 1825 at the age of twenty-one, and stayed until her retirement. Known as Julie, perhaps because there were already too many Carolines in the house, she entertained the young Gustave with stories; he, in turn, would ask her to help him write his first tales.

A Writer's Education

Even before his formal education had started, Gustave spent hours inventing stories and plays. His younger sister learned her letters before he did, and the family initially expressed some worry about his intellectual abilities. This fear that he could be intellectually slow was dissected at great length in Jean-Paul Sartre's controversial biography, *The Family Idiot*. Sartre's unfinished multivolume exploration of Flaubert's life took a decade to write and combines Marxist and Freudian analysis with Sartre's own hypotheses about the making of the great nineteenth-century writer.

But there is little proof that Flaubert was anything close to an "idiot." In his early childhood, he would sneak out of the garden and across the street to visit "le père Mignot," an elderly neighbor who read him stories. His favorite was an abridged version of Cervantes's *Don Quixote*, and he soon learned the story by heart. The tale stayed with him as an adult, and he kept a copy of the unabridged version beside his bed for regular reading. (His bedside copy of *Don Quixote* has been preserved, along with much of his library, and can be seen at the town hall of Canteleu, about five miles north of Rouen.)

By the age of eight, Flaubert was writing his own plays and stories. In 1832, his parents enrolled him at ❻ **the Collège Royal de Rouen** (now Lycée Corneille), **4 rue**

No image of Caroline Flaubert, Gustave's sister, survives other than this bust by sculptor James Pradier.

du Maulévrier. The former Jesuit college is now a well-regarded high school where cell phone–toting teens gather next to Corneille's statue in the well-preserved stone courtyard. The three-story stone building has an impressive portico, a spacious courtyard, and a large Baroque-style chapel.

Shortly before Gustave arrived at the school, with the overthrow of the Bourbon monarchy in 1830, the national curriculum changed from classical instruction mostly in Latin to more modern teachings in French. On August 1, 1830, Rouen marked the revolution by lowering the white fleur-de-lys emblem of the Bourbon kings from the Hôtel de Ville (city hall) and raising the national red, white, and blue of the tricolor. Louis-Philippe, a constitutional monarch who dressed like a businessman and carried an umbrella, rose to the throne. In Rouen, royal insignia were removed from public monuments and street signs. School discipline remained strict, however, with students following a military-like regime that included getting up at the crack of dawn and marching around in the freezing cold in orderly lines.

The school is scarcely a mile from the Hôtel Dieu, but at the time it was considered an important part of education to separate the young child from the family, so Flaubert was enrolled as a boarder. He was a brilliant student, although the austere atmosphere and strict discipline began to grate on him and would color his later writings about the period. His happy memories of the time related to his close ties to several teachers who noticed his talent for writing.

Flaubert fondly remembered the comradeship from his time at the large and austere school. Describing a cold day in winter, during which a small group of students were allowed to sit around a stove, he wrote: "We warmed ourselves lazily, we toasted our slices of bread on our rulers, the chimney was humming; we talked about everything under the sun: the plays we'd seen, the women we'd loved, leaving college, what we planned to do when we were grown up."

The entrance to the Lycée Corneille, formerly the Collège Royal de Rouen, where Flaubert—like Corneille before him and de Maupassant after him—came to study.

Many years later, Flaubert would begin *Madame Bovary* with a description of Charles Bovary starting school at his very own Collège Royal: "We were in study hall when the headmaster entered, followed by a new boy not yet in school uniform and by the handyman carrying a large desk. Their arrival disturbed the slumbers of some of us, but we all stood up in our places as though rising from our work."

From his first year as a student, Flaubert wrote incessantly. He published his first story at age fourteen in *Arts et progrès*, a magazine he founded with school friends. Two years later he published two stories in a local magazine while at the same time writing historical tales that he shared with friends and teachers. Of these early writings, roughly fifty have been preserved, including his first draft of *Sentimental Education*, which he rewrote and published much later in his life. He read Victor Hugo, Walter Scott, Montaigne, and Rabelais. As he grew older, he was attracted to Romantic writers such as Byron and Goethe and was fascinated by the Marquis de Sade.

From 1834 to 1839, Flaubert studied history with a teacher who inspired and encouraged him. Pierre Adolphe Chéruel had been a pupil of the great French historian Michelet, and he encouraged Flaubert to write essays that were later rewarded with school prizes. Chéruel

29

Charles Bovary's Rouen

During his medical studies, Charles Bovary lives on ❼ **the Rue Eau-de-Robec,** which was then a run-down part of town inhabited mainly by the city's leather workers. A small, polluted river flowed down the street at that time, but was later covered up. The neighborhood was considered a slum until relatively recently, when the city restored the half-timbered homes on the narrow, ancient streets. The city also rebuilt a small waterway, which now flows under hanging flower baskets along a street that is today one of the most quaint and picturesque in Rouen.

Several years later, Charles, now a doctor in the small fictional town of Yonville-l'Abbaye, brings his wife, Emma, to the theater in an attempt to cheer her up. Unaware that she had been carrying on an affair with the dapper bachelor Rodolphe, who had recently abandoned her, Charles takes her to see a rendition of Donizetti's *Lucia di Lammermoor*

at the Théâtre des Arts, which was then at the end of the Rue Grand-Pont, looking out over the river. That theater burned down in 1872, and its replacement was destroyed by a bomb at the end of World War II. In 1962, the city built a new theater several blocks to the west along the Quai Pierre Corneille.

A small waterway flows beneath hanging flowers on the Rue Eau-de-Robec today.

The Rue Eau-de-Robec, on a day when the street was dry.

pushed his students to seek the truth in history through rigorous research rather than emotional response. Flaubert was fascinated with antiquity and remarked that he felt as if he had once lived in another era. He wrote in his private journal in 1841 that he sometimes experienced such clear "historical revelations" that he believed he had seen events in a previous life.

Chéruel insisted, however, that his students do extensive background research to build a true picture of the past. Flaubert took that advice throughout his life when researching his historical writing; for instance, in April 1858, he traveled to Carthage to do research for his historical novel *Salammbô*. His teacher also helped ignite a lifelong attraction to the study of history. "I love history, madly. I find the dead more agreeable than the living," he exclaimed in a letter dated 1860. Flaubert never forgot Chéruel and sent him copies of all of his published writing.

Flaubert was a good student, but he lacked discipline, was known as a prankster, and could be feisty and combative. When a philosophy teacher punished a group of students —including Flaubert—for talking and creating disorder in class, the students initially refused the order to write out a thousand lines as punishment. The school administrators remained firm, and most of the students complied. Flaubert and a small group kept up their protest, however, and were expelled in 1839.

Because of his father's prestige, Flaubert was allowed to finish preparing for his baccalauréat exam at his family's hospital apartment. He passed the exam, but the seven years he spent at the school

influenced his life and work beyond this measure of academic success. He wrote little about the conflict that his expulsion might have caused in his family. In a letter to friend Ernest Chevalier, he explained:

> *If you want to hear some news, or at least a piece of the news, I can tell you that I am no longer at the college and since I am so weary of the details of my story and I'm just fed up with it I refer you to Alfred for the narrative. I am therefore going to work hard for my baccalauréat, though for the moment I am supremely lazy and all I do is sleep.*

Flaubert would soon leave Rouen. In the small garden outside the family's hospital apartment, near the walls where the young Flaubert climbed on trellises to spy on the corpses his father had dissected, there is a stone monument to the writer by sculptor Henri Chapu. Erected in 1890, just two years after Flaubert's death, the monument depicts Flaubert and the figure of a woman meant to represent *Madame Bovary*.

Rouen Friends

While a student, Flaubert met Louis Bouilhet, a poet and playwright who would later become a friend and intellectual compatriot so close that Flaubert called him "half my brain." Bouilhet was first a classmate at school, then a student of Flaubert's father, and finally Flaubert's closest friend for two

This stone monument to Flaubert adorns the wall of the garden of the Hôtel Dieu where he used to play with his sister.

decades. The friendship did not flourish until the two had long left the school, but their acquaintance served as a foundation for their extraordinarily close personal and working relationship.

Though Flaubert seemed not to care about his own stature in Rouen, he fought valiantly to preserve his friend's memory. After Bouilhet's death in 1869, Flaubert wrote a blistering letter to city authorities when they initially declined his request to build a monument to Bouilhet. Flaubert had offered to pay for the fountain and statue, and he was outraged when the city fathers rejected the proposal because Bouilhet was not born in their city and because his literary stature was not sufficiently grand. "Here was a man who in this century of great fortunes, dedicated his life to the cult of letters," Flaubert wrote in a letter to the city.

Bouilhet enjoyed some success during his lifetime, but he is best known now as the friend who encouraged and inspired Flaubert as he started work on *Madame Bovary* and successive novels. Flaubert called him his

Ernest Chevalier, who became attorney general of Angers, was a lifelong friend of Flaubert.

An 1831 letter from Flaubert to Ernest Chevalier.

literary midwife, and remained close to him to the end of his life. In *Souvenirs Intimes (Intimate Memories)*, Flaubert's niece, who was by then Caroline Franklin Grout, wrote about the close friendship. "He [Flaubert] would go for months on end seeing no one but his close friend Louis Bouilhet, who would come to visit on Sunday and stay until Monday. For part of the night, he would read his week's worth of writing out loud. What wonderful hours of conversing! There were loud cries and continual exclamations, disagreements over the rejection or acceptance of an epithet, reciprocal encouragement."

Bouilhet was born in the nearby town of Cany, but spent most of his life in Rouen. He lived near the Vieux Marché on the Rue des Bons-Enfants and then near the Collège Royal on the Rue Beauvoisine. Unlike Flaubert, who never held a job and lived his entire life on an income provided by his father, Bouilhet needed to work. He was named curator of the municipal library in 1867.

Flaubert's public tirade against Rouen's government was not entirely in vain. In 1882, thirteen years after Bouilhet's death and two years after Flaubert died, the city inaugurated a ❽ **monument to Bouilhet**—a bust above an ornate stone fountain—on the corner of what

Louis Bouilhet was a frequent visitor to the Flaubert home and such a close friend that Flaubert called him "half my brain."

Flaubert had to fight Rouen's city government to get them to build a monument to his friend.

33

is now **Rue Lecanuet and Rue Jacques-Villon**, near the library and the city's Museum of Fine Arts.

Bouilhet was buried near the Flaubert family plot at ❾ **the Cimetière Monumental**, on a hill looking down at the city. His poetry and plays have been largely forgotten, although he was well appreciated by his contemporaries. The writer Guy de Maupassant quotes Bouilhet's poetry in his short story "Found on a Drowned Man":

> I hate the poet who with tearful eye
> Murmurs some name while gazing tow'rds a star,
> Who sees no magic in the earth or sky,
> Unless Lizette or Ninon be not far.
>
> The bard who in all Nature nothing sees
> Divine, unless a petticoat he ties
> Amorously to the branches of the trees
> Or nightcap to the grass, is scarcely wise.
>
> He has not heard the Eternal's thunder tone,
> The voice of Nature in her various moods,
> Who cannot tread the dim ravines alone,
> And of no woman dream mid whispering woods.

Flaubert also renewed his friendship with another future poet, Alfred Le Poittevin, while a student at the Collège Royal. (Their mothers had known each other since their own childhoods, when they met as schoolgirls in Honfleur.) Although Le Poittevin was five years older than Flaubert, the two became close friends who wrote to one another often. "It is truly wrong for you and me to part, to disrupt our work and our intimacy," Flaubert wrote to Le Poittevin in April 1845, as he was getting ready to accompany his sister (with his parents) on her honeymoon trip to Italy. "Each time we have done so we have found ourselves the worse to it. Once again, at this last separation, I felt

a pang; it was less of a shock to me than other times, but still very depressing." Flaubert worshipped his older friend and sent him many manuscripts to read, valuing his opinion above all others. Le Poittevin's poetry no doubt inspired Flaubert and reflected themes and

Guy de Maupassant

I am still prostrated by this calamity, and his dear face follows me everywhere. His voice haunts me, phrases keep coming back, the disappearance of his affection seems to have emptied the world around me. At three-thirty in the afternoon on Saturday, May 8th, I received a telegram from Mme Commanville [Flaubert's niece, Caroline]: 'Flaubert apoplexy. No hope. Leaving at six.' I joined the Commanvilles at six o'clock at the station; but stopping at my apartment on the way I found two other telegrams from Rouen announcing his death. We made the horrible journey in the dark, sunk in black and cruel grief. At Croisset we found him on his bed, looking almost unchanged, except that his neck was dark and swollen from the apoplexy.
—Guy de Maupassant, writing to Ivan Turgenev to inform him of Flaubert's death, May 25, 1880

Guy de Maupassant's letter to the Russian writer describes the circumstances of Flaubert's sudden death from apoplexy, or stroke. It also reveals the affectionate and close relationship between the older writer and his Norman disciple.

De Maupassant, considered the greatest French short story writer, was born in 1850 in the northern Norman port of Dieppe. His mother, Laure Le Poittevin, was the sister of Flaubert's dear friend Alfred, and had herself known the writer since her childhood. Laure separated from her husband, Gustave de Maupassant, and raised her two sons, Guy and Hervé, alone. During this time, she kept in touch with

interests, such as his attraction to the East and antiquity, that he would later develop himself.

Flaubert was shattered when Le Poittevin married in 1846, and he mourned the occasion as a sort of death of

his close friendship with the poet. Flaubert equated marriage with giving in to the bourgeois lifestyle, a middle road that killed creativity. Le Poittevin went on to die in his thirties in 1848, and Flaubert maintained close ties with his sister, Laure, for most of his life.

Guy de Maupassant, a prolific writer and fellow Norman, was a family friend who relied on Flaubert for both literary advice and fatherly affection.

Flaubert. He sent her a copy of his novel *Salammbô* when it was published in 1862, and she read it aloud to her children after dinner.

Guy, twenty-nine years Flaubert's junior, attended the Collège Royal de Rouen and started to write as a student there. De Maupassant regularly brought Flaubert his poems and stories for review, and the two developed a friendship that lasted until Flaubert's death. De Maupassant volunteered to serve in the Franco-Prussian War at the age of twenty, and after returning to Paris he joined Flaubert's literary circle, which included Emile Zola and Turgenev. Despite his literary talents, he worked as a civil servant for much of his life, first at the ministry of maritime affairs, and then at the ministry of education.

During this time he also wrote nearly three hundred short stories, six novels, three travel books, and frequent newspaper articles. Influenced by Flaubert as well as by the naturalist movement led by Zola, de Maupassant wrote about what he knew best: rural Normandy, the Franco-Prussian War, office life in Paris, Parisian high society, and prostitution. Many of his stories set up a fictional situation in which one character tells the story, whether it be a journey on a train, an encounter, a courtroom speech, or a suicide note. His stories are largely pessimistic but reveal his sympathy for the downtrodden.

Near the end of his life in February 1880, Flaubert wrote to de Maupassant to congratulate him on "Boule de Suif" ("Ball of Fat"), the

story of a prostitute. "I'm impatient to tell you I consider 'Boule de Suif' a masterpiece," Flaubert wrote. "This little story will live: you can be sure of it." Flaubert was right: de Maupassant's work did stand the test of time. But he was also successful during his own brief lifetime and was eventually able to give up his civil service work.

Shortly before he died, Flaubert had given a photograph of himself to de Maupassant with an inscription saying he loved him like a son. Some hypothesized that de Maupassant could in fact be Flaubert's son, although the date on his birth certificate and other circumstances have quieted that theory. The two did, however, share one of the era's scourges: syphilis. De Maupassant died at forty-three, a victim of general paresis, a breakdown of mental function caused by damage to the brain from untreated syphilis. Flaubert's death could also have been hastened by syphilis, although he had a milder version and was spared the prolonged suffering that the disease could cause.

The Flaubert family's first country home was in Déville-lès-Rouen.

baggy trousers, gazes with nonchalance southward toward the cathedral.

While the Flauberts considered themselves Rouennais, they spent most summers at the beach at Trouville, in the countryside around Pont-l'Evêque, and at their country home at nearby Déville-lès-Rouen. But train tracks for a new line linking Rouen and Le Havre ran straight through the property, and Dr. Flaubert sold that house—to the east of the city—in August 1843. Only its outside staircase remains today.

Flaubert's connection to his friend continued when Laure married Gustave de Maupassant several years later, and shortly thereafter gave birth to a son, Guy.

Guy de Maupassant enrolled at the Collège Royal in 1868, and Flaubert took him under his wing when he saw the boy's promise as a writer.

Guy's mother lived on the Rue de l'Ecole at the time, and Flaubert and Bouilhet visited her often. Rouen's monument to Flaubert stands nearby in the small ❿ Place des Carmes. The statue is a copy of an original by the Russian sculptor Leopold Bernstamm, which was destroyed during World War II. The modest statue in the small, quiet square, compared to the large and prominent one of Corneille in front of the Théâtre des Arts beside the river, reflects the complex relationship Flaubert had with Rouen, especially during his lifetime. Flaubert, wearing a square waistcoat and

In April 1844, the family bought a country house on the outskirts of Rouen in the village of Croisset. The large, white eighteenth-century house looked out on the Seine and what was then pastoral countryside just northwest of the city. But the family's happy life was about to change drastically. That same year, Gustave had his first epileptic attack, leading him to abandon law studies in Paris for the calm of Croisset. Just two years later, his father died from an infected wound on his thigh, and several months later Flaubert's sister, Caroline, died of childbirth complications.

Flaubert retreated with his mother and infant niece to Croisset while his older brother, Achille, stayed on in the hospital apartment. From then until his death, Flaubert considered Croisset his home, although he had close friends in Rouen and continued to visit regularly. And even though he continued to criticize the city's

this time, and the two maintained an energetic correspondence that touched on politics, literature, and family. Sand and Flaubert bemoaned the political trends of the time and the increasing belligerence of nation-states such as Prussia.

In 1870–71, victorious Prussian troops moved into the house at Croisset. Flaubert and his mother fled to apartments on the Quai du Havre in Rouen, just south of the Vieux Marché. To Flaubert's surprise, the soldiers did little damage to his house (other than leaving a lingering smell of boot leather), and he returned as soon as they left.

A Meeting at the Cathedral

The Cathédrale Notre-Dame defines the skyline of Rouen and has always added to the city's sense of pride. It has also been the target of attackers over the centuries.

Most recently, on the night of April 18, 1944, 345 Allied bombs fell from the sky onto the old city. The bombs set rows of medieval houses on fire and also hit the seven-hundred-year-old cathedral, crushing the organ and pounding the side chapels and flying buttresses. Then, in May, the cathedral was hit again when an unexploded bomb detonated, setting fire to the Saint-Romain tower. Just as the flames subsided there, a nearby church, ❶ the Eglise Saint-Maclou, on the **Place Barthélémy**, was ripped apart by bombs. When the Canadians finally arrived on August 30, they found a largely ruined city. Since then, however, Rouen has restored its medieval center and its many churches, including the Cathédrale Notre-Dame.

inhabitants, he liked to show the city off to visiting friends. In 1866, the writer George Sand came to visit and wrote this in her diary: "I arrived in Rouen at one o'clock. Found Flaubert waiting at the station with a carriage. He showed me around the town and the sights: the cathedral, the city hall, Saint-Maclou, Saint-Patrice: marvelous. An old graveyard and some ancient streets: very quaint."

Near the end of his life, although he enjoyed visiting the literary salons of Paris, Flaubert lived a relatively quiet life in Croisset with his mother. His friendship with the much-older George Sand had blossomed by

Flaubert knew the city's churches and cathedral well and used them often as inspiration and settings for his writing. When Emma and her lover, Léon, meet at the cathedral at a crucial scene in *Madame Bovary*, Flaubert writes, "The church was like a gigantic boudoir, suffused by her image. . . ." Emma appears, starts to pray, and then takes a guided tour before Léon sweeps her away into a covered carriage for a tour of Rouen, but one during which she will see nothing at all of the city.

Where do they want to go, the driver asks. "Anywhere," Léon responds. The carriage takes off on an undirected lovers' journey. The ride takes the two to every corner of the town: up the hill to the Cimetière Monumental and past several of the town's churches—Saint-Romain, Saint-Vivien, Saint-Maclou, Saint-Nicaise. When the driver tries to stop at a café to get a drink, the two lovers protest, and he lashes the horses and forges ahead, "demoralized, and almost weeping from thirst, fatigue and despair."

Along the river front amidst the trucks and the barrels, along the streets from the shelter of the guard posts, the bourgeois stared wide-eyed at this spectacle unheard of in the provinces—a carriage with drawn shades that kept appearing and reappearing, sealed tighter than a tomb and tossing like a ship.

Hours later, "at about six o'clock, the carriage stopped in a side street near ❷ **the Place Beauvoisine.** A woman alighted from it and walked off, her veil down, without a backward glance."

The cathedral's cast-iron spire replaced one made from wood and lead, making it the tallest church steeple in France.

The great cathedral's construction spanned several centuries, and its combination of styles and eras illustrates the city's tumultuous history. The first Romanesque cathedral was built and consecrated in 1063 by Archbishop Maurille in the presence of William the Conqueror, just three years before his forces invaded England. Construction on a rib-vaulted cathedral started in the following century; the Tour Saint-Romain had just been completed when a fire broke out in the year 1200 and destroyed the entire edifice. It was rebuilt during the following thirty years in Norman Gothic style, and much of the cathedral that remains today dates from that time.

Work was far from done, however: chapels were added to the aisles in the fourteenth century, and the frontal tower known as the Tour du Beurre (Butter Tower) dates from the fifteenth century. (It owes its name to the popular belief that it had been paid for in exchange for a dispensation to eat butter and drink milk during Lent.) The central Lantern Tower was finished in 1517.

Inside the cathedral, a stained glass window in the north transept that dates from the thirteenth century tells the story of Saint Julian in thirty-four panels. In his story "The Legend of Saint Julian the Hospitator," one of three in his collection *Three Tales*, Flaubert tells the story of Julian, whose parents believe he is destined to become an emperor or a saint. A child hunter, Julian one day massacres an entire valley full of deer, and a stag curses him to kill his own parents. He flees to escape his future, much like Oedipus. Eventually he marries a princess, travels, and upon return from a trip finds two bodies asleep in his bed. Thinking his wife has been unfaithful, he kills the two, only to find that they were his sleeping parents, come to pay him a visit. As penance, he gives up his belongings and lives the life of a beggar, helps a leper who turns out to be an angel, and is taken to heaven. "And there is the story

of saint Julien H, as it is told in a stained glass window of a church in my country," Flaubert concludes his short story.

For the last story in this collection, "Herodias," Flaubert took the dance of Salomé, which is portrayed in the tympanum above the cathedral's Saint John door, as inspiration for his retelling of the beheading of John the Baptist. The stone carving, also completed in the thirteenth century, refers to the story of Saint John the Baptist, with Salomé dancing below. The scene portrayed in the tympanum sets the scene for Flaubert's story. "Then she began to dance," Flaubert writes in the story. "Her feet moved rhythmically one in front of the other to the sounds of a flute and a pair of hand cymbals. She extended her arms in a circle, as if she were calling to someone who was fleeing her approach."

In the nineteenth century, an architect named Alavoine replaced the wood and lead of the central tower with a cast-iron spire, making it the tallest church steeple in France. Just as the building of the Eiffel Tower had created a stir and drawn much criticism, irate Rouennais—including Flaubert—protested the modernization. Flaubert called the addition "grotesque" and compared it to putting an "oblong cage" atop his beloved cathedral. It is easy to imagine what these critics would have thought of the evening light and music show that now regularly transforms the historic monument into a flashing, twenty-first-century spectacle.

A City for Flaubert Scholars

In 1914, Flaubert's niece and sole heir, Caroline Franklin Grout, gave Rouen's ⑬ **Bibliothèque Municipale, at 3 rue Jacques-Villon,** an important gift: the original manuscripts of *Madame Bovary* and his last, unfinished novel, *Bouvard and Pécuchet*. His manuscripts, full of crossed-out and rewritten passages, reveal his obsession with style and finding just the right word.

The library has since added more documents and manuscripts relating to Flaubert and attracts a steady stream of Flaubert scholars from around the world. The library, which displays a portrait of Flaubert in the stairway leading to the research area, is a part of the same building that houses the Museum of Fine Arts. The museum's collection includes works by famous painters, including Caravaggio, Delacroix, Modigliani, Monet, and Sisley; it also features works by the painter Joseph-Désiré Court, most notably a portrait of a young lady that is often thought to represent Emma Bovary (although this has never been proven) and that has been used as cover art for dozens of editions of the novel. Court was a sort of official portrait artist for the Flaubert family, and several of his paintings can also be seen at the Musée Flaubert at the Hôtel Dieu in Rouen.

The city that once ignored Flaubert's funeral procession now, in addition to creating museums and building monuments to his greatness, also promotes and welcomes scholarship surrounding Flaubert and other notable writers born there. The Association of Friends of Flaubert and de Maupassant organizes meetings and lectures relating to the lives and work of the two Norman writers at its headquarters at the Hôtel des Sociétés Savantes on the Rue Beauvoisine.

And in the adjacent suburb of Mont-Saint-Aignan, Flaubert scholar Yvan Leclerc directs the Flaubert Center at the University of Rouen, which was founded in 1966. Leclerc created and helps maintain a website (www.univ-rouen.fr/flaubert/index.htm) that links Flaubert scholars, students, collectors, and researchers from around the world and has become a trove of commentary, documents, translations, and images related to Flaubert's life and work.

A rough draft of *Madame Bovary* displays Flaubert's propensity for rewriting.

Chapter 3
Trouville
Footprints in the Sand

Eugène Boudin, *The Beach at Trouville* (1865).

In my youth I loved immeasurably, a love that was unrequited, intense and silent. Nights spent gazing at the moon, dreaming of elopements and travels in Italy, dreams of glory for her sake, torments of the body and soul, spasms at the smell of a shoulder, and turning suddenly pale when I caught her eye, I have known all that, and known it very well. Each one of us has in his heart a royal chamber. I have had mine bricked up, but it is still there.

—Flaubert, letter to his friend
Amélie Bosquet, 1859

In July 1836, Flaubert met the love of his life, Elisa Schlesinger. He was fourteen, a schoolboy vacationing with his family at a fishing village on the Normandy coast. She was a twenty-five-year-old mother of an infant, visiting the seaside town with the baby's father. According to his autobiographical novel *Memoirs of a Madman*, written when he was sixteen, he found the woman's fur-lined cloak lying on the damp sand and moved it to a drier part of the beach. She noticed the gesture and thanked her young admirer while he was having lunch with his family at the inn in Trouville, where they were staying. He later saw her nursing her baby and nearly swooned at the sight of her naked breast.

Trouville would live on in Flaubert's memory largely because of his meeting with Elisa. The young Flaubert got to know Elisa and Maurice Schlesinger that summer, engaging them in conversation and accompanying them on walks along Trouville's paths and vast beach. It is unlikely that the young mother knew his feelings for her at the time, but neither she nor Maurice seemed to mind his company.

Elisa Schlesinger, Gustave's first love and lifelong acquaintance, with her daughter, Marie.

beachside resort town an important landmark throughout his life.

Elisa Schlesinger was born Elisa Foucault on September 23, 1810, in Vernon, a Norman town thirty-five miles upstream along the Seine from Rouen. She had been married at the age of nineteen to a junior military officer, but later separated from him before he left for duty in Africa. She soon met Maurice Schlesinger and had a child, although it is not clear whether they were legally married during the summer of 1836. Flaubert, unaware of these details, was taken with the seductive older woman, even though he realized that a romantic relationship with her was pure fantasy. He described her beauty in his autobiographical novella:

She was tall, dark, with magnificent black hair that fell in tresses on her shoulders; her nose was Greek, her eyes burning, her eyebrows high and admirably arched, her skin was ardent and seemed coated with gold; she was slender and delicate, and there were blue veins climbing her brown and crimson neck.

The Trouville meeting and Flaubert's fierce but unrequited love would have an influence that carried on well after the summer vacation. Elisa would be the model for several of his fictional characters, starting with Maria in *Memoirs of a Madman*, and ultimately also for the older Madame Arnoux in his coming-of-age novel *Sentimental Education*. The memory of his first meeting with Elisa, with whom he kept in touch until her death in a German mental hospital, made the

Even after the family beach holidays ceased, Flaubert remained nostalgic about Trouville, which he equated with youth and his first passion. He returned to the beach resort years later in 1853, and wrote to his lover, Louise Colet, "I cannot take a step without running upon some youthful memory. Each wave as it breaks

Flaubert's Affairs

Even though he idealized his early love, Elisa Schlesinger, for much of his life, Flaubert had an active love life that he described in detail in letters to friends. His sexual initiation started soon after his Trouville passion for Elisa. With coaxing from his older friend Alfred Le Poittevin, Flaubert began to visit Rouen prostitutes. (Brothels proliferated in France during the nineteenth century, in part because large numbers of rural women migrated to cities to find low-wage work in factories and were easily lured into prostitution. What's more, the decade following the July Revolution of 1830 saw a relaxation of the censorious mores that had prevailed under the Bourbon rulers, and young men were more open about visiting brothels.)

Just as they shunned the bourgeois convention of marriage, Flaubert and his male friends considered their interest in prostitutes a rebellion against middle-class society. "I love prostitution for itself, independently of what it offers," Flaubert wrote to Louise Colet in June 1853. "In the very notion of prostitution there is such a complex convergence of lust and bitterness, such a frenzy of muscle and sound of gold. . . . Yes, he who has never woken up in a nameless bed, who has never seen sleeping on his pillow a face he will never see again, is missing a great deal."

Fascination with prostitutes also had its downside. Like many of his friends, Flaubert suffered from the symptoms of (and treatment for) syphilis for much of his life. In his *Dictionary of Accepted Ideas*, he defines the illness as a common malady: "Syphilis: Everybody has it, more or less." The standard treatment at the time was mercury, which often produced uncomfortable side effects, including excessive salivation, intestinal problems, rashes, and discoloration of the teeth.

Despite his periodic health problems, Flaubert carried on numerous affairs. As a young man he was tall, blond, and described as an Adonis. (He avoided having his portrait painted at all costs, however, so there are no images of him from the era to verify this description.) Even as he lost his hair and put on weight, he remained attractive to women. He remained firm in his resolve never to marry, however, as he was sure marriage would stifle his creativity.

Friends continued to remind him, though, that the solitary life came with costs. Writing to Flaubert in 1872, George Sand suggested that he marry to alleviate his loneliness and gloomy mood. "Living for oneself is a bad thing," Sand wrote. By that time, Flaubert replied, he felt himself too poor and too old to make such a radical change. "The feminine existence has never fitted in with mine," he wrote.

Degas' *Party at the Brothel* (1878–79).

A Chronological—but Incomplete—List of Flaubert's Loves

Elisa Schlesinger: Unrequited and idealized love. Flaubert met the older Elisa on the beach in Trouville when he was just fourteen. She became the model for Madame Arnoux in *Sentimental Education*, and Flaubert stayed in touch with her for the rest of her life.

Eulalie Foucaud: An erotic awakening. After graduating from school in 1840, Flaubert received a gift from his parents: a Grand Tour south to the Mediterranean in the company of Dr. Jules Cloquet, a good friend of his parents. In Marseille, Flaubert met a dark-haired thirty-five-year-old who, with her mother, ran the Hôtel de Richelieu on the Rue de la Darse. They spent only one night together, but amorous letters followed and Flaubert never forgot her, although they lost touch over the years. Eighteen years after their tryst, Flaubert made a pilgrimage to find the hotel, only to discover that the building now housed a bazaar and a barbershop.

Louise Colet: True love? For eight years, Flaubert carried on an affair that was his longest and most serious romantic involvement. Early on, however, he warned the poet that he would break her heart. In the end, Flaubert could not commit to a long-term relationship with his demanding lover, and in 1855 he broke it off. Colet was bitterly disappointed. When she died in 1876, Flaubert said he was saddened by the news.

Kuchiuk-Hanem: An Egyptian fantasy. Flaubert met this exotic courtesan in 1850 on a trip down the Nile with friend Maxime Du Camp. She lived in the town of Esna, notorious as the site to which well-known Cairo prostitutes and dancers had been banished by the mullahs. After a night of vigorous partying, dancing, and sex, Flaubert lay down next to her to go to sleep. "I scarcely shut my eyes," Flaubert wrote to Louis Bouilhet. "My night was one long, infinitely intense reverie." Flaubert never forgot Kuchiuk-Hanem, and he recounted his experience with her to many friends and lovers, including Louise Colet, who on a trip to Egypt much later tried unsuccessfully to find the courtesan.

Juliet Herbert: Secret love. Juliet Herbert was the English governess who came to Croisset to take care of Flaubert's niece, Caroline, in 1853. Flaubert's biographers agree that she later became Flaubert's lover, although details of the affair are not clear.

reawakens within me impressions of long ago. I hear a roar of days that are past, and an unending surge, like the surge of the sea, of vanished emotions."

Warriors' Town

When the Flauberts first started coming to Trouville in the 1830s, the fishing village was not yet widely popular as a vacation spot, but it had a long history as a fishing port and a landing site for invaders. The city was founded in the ninth century by a Viking invader named Thorulfr, which means "Thor's wolf." Thorulfr founded a domain known as Thorulfvilla, or "Thor's wolf's estate," and the name evolved over the years to become Trouville.

The town owes its development as a fishing village and then as a bustling resort town to its geographic position on the English Channel—or "La Manche" (the sleeve) as the French call it—and along the Touques River, which provided an easy path for communications with the interior of the region, known as the Pays d'Auge. Surrounding forests added to its appeal and strategic location by providing timber for boat building and animals for hunting.

Even after the Vikings had come and gone, warriors continued to arrive at Trouville, especially during the Hundred Years' War. The period of strife between France and England began in 1337 when Edward III, allied with the nobles of the Low Countries and the burghers of Flanders, rallied his troops for a period of domination over the French. In July 1346, Edward mounted a major invasion across the Channel, landing on the Cotentin peninsula and marching across Normandy. His armies laid waste to the region, but in 1348 the plague began to sweep across Europe, preventing England from launching any major offenses. After the plague had subsided, France under the reign of Charles V was able to push back English advances during the end of the fourteenth century. But when Henry V took the throne in England at the start of the fifteenth century, he began a new period of attacks on France and Normandy in particular. His most famous foray culminated in 1415 in the battle of Agincourt, memorably described in Shakespeare's play *Henry V*.

Shakespeare and Flaubert

Throughout Flaubert's life he read, reread, and discussed with friends the great books of writers such as Cervantes, Montaigne, and Voltaire. But one great writer rose above the rest for him: Shakespeare. "He was not a man, he was a continent," Flaubert wrote to Louise Colet in September 1852. "He contained whole crowds of great men, entire landscapes. Writers like him do not worry about style: they are powerful in spite of all their faults and because of them." (In an earlier letter to Colet, Flaubert had written, "The three finest things God ever made are the sea, 'Hamlet' and Mozart's 'Don Giovanni.'")

Flaubert read and reread Shakespeare throughout his life. This edition of Shakespeare plays comes from Flaubert's library, which now resides in the town hall in Canteleu, near his family's former home in Croisset.

Shakespeare's history *Henry V* tells the story of the king who played such an important role in Normandy's history. The play follows Henry V's campaign, which began in the town of Harfleur in August 1415. His forces raided across France toward Calais in an expedition that culminated in the battle of Agincourt, north of the Somme River.

For Flaubert, however, it was *Hamlet* that most captured his imagination. In particular, he admired Shakespeare's ability to create a character full of inconsistency. "His perpetual state of fluctuation, his constant uncertainty, his irresolution, and his inability to resolve his thoughts—these are what makes the play sublime," he wrote to Louise Colet in June 1853, in the middle of composing *Madame Bovary*, a portrait of a woman who was herself tortured by complex and changing emotions. "The truth is that Shakespeare's conception of Hamlet reaches into the remotest corners of the human soul."

In 1417, Henry V arrived at Trouville's estuary, followed by 238 ships and 10,000 men, to retake the region. The château-fort of Touques, several miles upstream from the port, was besieged for thirteen days before it fell to Henry's army; only ruins remain today. Henry V went on to take much of Normandy, including Caen and Rouen.

Henry died in 1422, leaving an infant son who would be crowned Henry VI of England and also king of France, but much of France remained loyal to Charles VI's son, and after the appearance of Joan of Arc, the tide of war began to turn. By 1449, the French had retaken Rouen. Normandy—and France—had been devastated by the years of war, but French nationalism had been awakened. In the end, the Hundred Years' War helped accelerate France's transformation from a feudal monarchy to a centralized state.

Escape from the City

They almost always rested in the same field, with Deauville on their left, and Le Havre on their right, and the open sea in front. The water glittered in the sunshine, smooth as a mirror, and so still that the murmur it made was scarcely audible; unseen sparrows could be heard

A sketch of the beach at Trouville from 1845.

twittering, and the sky covered the whole scene with its huge canopy.

—Flaubert, "A Simple Heart"

When the Flaubert family started vacationing in Trouville, they had to work hard to get there. The town was only about ten miles from Pont-l'Evêque but they made the trip on foot, with horses carrying their belongings, and the voyage from Rouen took several days. Flaubert re-created that trip in his short story "A Simple Heart," which he wrote at the age of fifty-six as a tribute both to his mother's native region and to his aging friend and fellow writer George Sand, who had urged him to show his softer side.

In the story, the maid Félicité sets off for Trouville with the family she works for—Madame Aubain and her two children, Paul and Virginie, characters meant to represent Flaubert and his younger sister as children. To get ready for the trip, Madame Aubain "made preparations as if for a long journey." Then, the day before the departure, she sends the luggage off in a farm wagon. Finally, the family and their maid climb onto their horses' saddles, with the young son riding a donkey, to make the five-mile journey. "The road was so bad that the five-mile journey took them two hours," the story recounts. And that was just to a farm, where the family rests along the way. "The horses sank up to their pasterns in the mud and lurched forward in order to pull themselves free." The caravan then continues on to Trouville, where they settle in at L'Agneau d'Or (the Golden Lamb).

The Flaubert family stayed at ❶ **L'Agneau d'Or**, at the corner of what is now the **Rue de Verdun and the Boulevard Fernand Moureaux**—at the time one of the few local inns, and also favored by Alexandre Dumas.

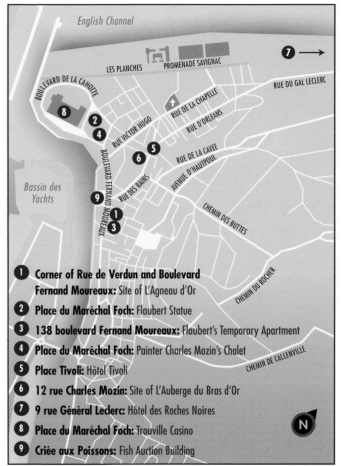

❶ **Corner of Rue de Verdun and Boulevard Fernand Moureaux:** Site of L'Agneau d'Or

❷ **Place du Maréchal Foch:** Flaubert Statue

❸ **138 boulevard Fernand Moureaux:** Flaubert's Temporary Apartment

❹ **Place du Maréchal Foch:** Painter Charles Mozin's Chalet

❺ **Place Tivoli:** Hôtel Tivoli

❻ **12 rue Charles Mozin:** Site of L'Auberge du Bras d'Or

❼ **9 rue Général Leclerc:** Hôtel des Roches Noires

❽ **Place du Maréchal Foch:** Trouville Casino

❾ **Criée aux Poissons:** Fish Auction Building

(The inn has since been torn down and replaced, like most of the town's buildings that dated from the early eighteenth century.) Flaubert spent his days, much as his characters Paul and Virginie did, wandering the beach and the cliffs that rose above the water.

The Flaubert family returned for several summers. In 1842, taking a break from law studies in Paris, Flaubert came to meet his family in Trouville and described his

Early morning low tide reveals black rocks that cover the sand beneath jagged bluffs.

joy at rediscovering the place. "I arrived, on foot, in wonderful moonlight, at three in the morning. I can still remember the canvas jacket and the stick I was carrying and the exhilaration I felt when I caught the salt smell of the distant sea."

Flaubert later resurrected these memories of the uncomplicated pleasures of eating, sleeping, walking the beach, and gazing at the sea in "A Simple Heart":

In the afternoon, they would take the donkey and walk out beyond the Roches Noires, towards Hennequeville. At first the path wound up between gently rolling meadows like the lawn in a park and then came to a plateau where there were grazing pastures and ploughed fields. The path was lined with holly bushes which grew amongst the tangle of brambles, and here and there the branches of a large dead tree traced their zigzag patterns against the blue of the sky.

The *roches noires* (black rocks) still appear at low tide on a section of the beach that is separated from the main stretch of sand and development by a small peninsula, which is now home to a modest yacht club. While the town itself has changed greatly since Flaubert's time, the black rocks and the paths above the beach have remained largely untouched. At high tide, the water obscures the scattering of black rocks that cover the beach for more than a mile when the tide pulls back. Shrimp fishermen troll the shallow waters with a type of low-tech fishing net that has changed little over the years, and artists set up their easels to paint the wide seascape and jagged bluffs.

Children's games on the beach haven't changed much either. "At other times they would take the ferry across the Touques and go looking for shells. At low tide, sea urchins, ormers and jellyfish were left behind on the land. The children would chase after flecks of foam blown about by the breeze."

In the years following the July Revolution of 1830, with the fall of the Bourbon monarchy and King Louis-

Philippe's establishment of a constitutional monarchy, France's bourgeoisie became increasingly prosperous. Known as the Citizen King, Louis-Philippe—who reigned until the next "revolution," in 1848—ushered in a period of ascendancy for members of the propertied classes such as the Flauberts. Prosperous citizens now had the time and the means to spend weeks at newly fashionable resorts such as Trouville, and writers and artists recorded their scenes of leisure. They also had an easier time getting there, as railway lines were built from Paris to the coast.

This period also corresponded with Dr. and Mrs. Flaubert's growing interest in buying property. They already owned a country home in the village of Déville, just outside of Rouen, and they added to their holdings

A lone painter stands at his easel on the empty Trouville beach.

in 1837 when they bought a farm in Deauville. The couple also owned the Ferme de Geffosses at Pont-l'Evêque, and they kept adding acreage to their farms and properties over the years. Most of their properties were rented out to farmers, producing substantial income over time. They never owned property in Trouville itself, but the city now considers the writer one of its own. A statue of Flaubert, in his typical nonchalant pose, wearing waistcoat and trousers, stands with his back to the Touques at ❷ **the Place du Maréchal Foch.**

Trouville Friends

After the summer of 1836, the Flauberts kept returning to Trouville, but Flaubert never saw his beloved Elisa there again. He continued to make friends on the beach, however, in particular two daughters of a British naval officer, Gertrude and Henriette Collier. Their father had lost money in a bank failure and fled to France, where life was cheaper at the time. Gertrude Collier, later to become Gertrude Tennant, would remain in touch with her friend throughout their lives. She described him during one of those summers: "At the time Gustave Flaubert looked like a young Greek. He was in mid-adolescence, tall and slender, lithe, and graceful as an athlete."

Henriette Collier was also enamored of the young, athletic Gustave. As a law student in Paris, he would stop by their Champs-Elysées apartment and read to them from his recent writings. Flaubert—writing to his longtime lover Louise Colet—describes one such meeting with Henriette in Paris, and his horror when she looked at him lovingly:

One day we were alone, sitting on a sofa; she took my hand, twined her fingers in mine; this I let her

do without thinking (most of the time I'm a great innocent), and she gave me a look which still makes me shiver. Just then her mother entered, took in everything, and smiled at what she thought was the acquisition of a son-in-law. . . . You cannot conceive the terror I felt.

As Mrs. Tennant, Gertrude would go on to become known for hosting parties featuring well-known writers and politicians in her London townhouse. Just five months before his death in 1880, Flaubert would write to her about his difficulties in making progress on his novel *Bouvard and Pécuchet.* The aging, tired-out writer presents a sharp contrast to the vital "young Greek" that Gertrude had met on the beach of Trouville.

Women figure very little, and love not at all. . . . I think the public won't have much understanding of it. People who read a book to discover whether the Baroness marries the Viscount will be disappointed, but I am writing for a few special spirits. Perhaps it will be a heavy-handed bit of foolishness? Or, on the contrary, something quite strong? I have no idea. And I am riddled with doubts and utterly exhausted.

Ghosts of Trouville

In August 1853, Flaubert returned to Trouville after many years to spend a few weeks at the beach with his mother and his niece Caroline, or "Liline," as he called her. He stayed at a friend's apartment above a pharmacy at ❸ **138 boulevard Fernand Moureaux** and spent his time wandering the beach and exploring his old haunts. He wrote to Louise Colet about his adolescent days and his passion for Elisa Schlesinger. Louise wrote back, complaining jealously about his "Trouville ghosts." He had already taunted her in a letter earlier in their relationship, writing of his love for Elisa, "I had only one true passion."

Flaubert was certainly never faithful to the memory of his unrequited love for Elisa, but he kept in touch with her and celebrated her in his writing. He called on the couple while studying law in Paris, and corresponded with them after they moved to Baden-Baden, where Elisa suffered from mental illness and spent some time in an institution. From all accounts, Maurice Schlesinger never objected to Flaubert's admiration for his wife. In 1871, Flaubert learned that Maurice had died, and he wrote to Elisa perhaps more freely about his memories of their youthful meeting. "For me, the sand on Trouville beach still holds your footprints," he proclaimed.

The following year, Flaubert wrote to her again. "I can never see your handwriting without being shaken. So this morning I eagerly tore open the envelope of your letter," he wrote on October 5, 1872. He told her that she would be welcome to come and stay at Croisset—his mother had died and left an empty bedroom—and describes his sadness at growing old and losing his friends and the comfort that his home still afforded him:

> Paris is no longer Paris; all my friends are dead; those who remain count for little, or are so changed that I no longer recognize them. . . .
>
> I have been given a dog. I take him for walks, watch the effect of the sun on the

Elisa Schlesinger as an old lady.

Monet's Trouville

In June 1870, Claude Monet married Camille Doncieux, his lover for the previous five years. The couple already had a son, Jean, and had lived together in Paris in near poverty. That summer, the Monet family went to Trouville to visit friend and fellow painter Eugène Boudin, fifteen years Monet's senior and famous for his blustery scenes and portraits of women on the beach. The seaside idyll, during which Monet produced a series of studies of Camille on the wide, sandy beach, took place at the same time as the start of the Franco-Prussian War. One painting, *The Beach at Trouville,* captures at once a breezy scene at the beach and an ominous foreshadowing of tense times ahead. The faces of the two women are indistinct; Camille's eye is a brown triangle on a smeared face. While Camille is dressed all in white, Madame Boudin looks severe in black hat and dress. There are actual grains of sand on the canvas, proving that Monet painted at least some of it while on the beach.

Boudin had been an important influence on Monet's evolving painting style. The two had met in 1858 in Le Havre, and Boudin had encouraged his young protégé to start painting outdoors. Monet would later declare, "If I have become a painter, I owe it all to Eugène Boudin." After their summer in Trouville, Monet fled with his family to London to avoid conscription. Soon after, Prussians occupied Normandy.

Monet's *The Beach at Trouville* (1870) is one of five beach scenes he produced that summer.

Sun worshippers and sea bathers gather on the beach at Trouville today.

yellowing leaves, and like an old man dream of the past—for I am an old man. For me the future no longer holds dreams, but the days of the past seem as though bathed in golden light. Against the background of the light, beloved phantoms reach out to me: and the face that stands out most splendidly is—yours. Yes, yours. Oh, poor dear Trouville!

Parisians Come to Play

After the invasions and strife of the Hundred Years' War had subsided, the Normandy coast enjoyed several centuries of comparative peace. Until the nineteenth century, Trouville was a sleepy fishing village that was difficult to reach. The picturesque town, which sits across the river from sister city Deauville, got its start as an artistic destination in the early nineteenth

century when the painter Charles Mozin arrived and began his series of seascapes and beach scenes.

Unlike other artists who had come and gone before, Mozin settled in at Trouville and made it his primary residence. The painter, whose ❹ chalet stills stands on the **Place Maréchal Foch,** was said to have "discovered" Trouville as an artistic and tourist destination. Shortly after Mozin, French painters Paul Huet and Eugène Isabey followed, and in the mid-1860s Gustave Courbet came to stay. Shortly after, in 1870, Claude Monet brought his wife and son to spend the summer in Trouville, staying at ❺ **the Hôtel Tivoli,** on the **Place Tivoli.**

The parade of artists and writers helped to spread the word in Paris, Rouen, and other nearby cities about Trouville as an unspoiled vacation spot. Alexandre

A Frightful Sight

In the 1830s, the normally heavily dressed French began to strip down and bathe in the sea. It was considered to be good for one's health. The Flauberts were no exception; they thought the water would be good for their daughter, Caroline, who was frail and often sick. The fad has continued over the years with the development of spas along the coast. Until recently, the French could get free spa treatments with a note from their doctor.

Flaubert, upon his return to Trouville as an adult in 1853, was appalled by the new fashions and lack of modesty displayed by the adventurous bathers of the time. In a letter written during this stay, he described the scene and his distaste for the spectacle: "I spent an hour yesterday watching the ladies bathe. What a sight! What a hideous sight!" In the past, he noted, the two sexes had bathed together, but they were now kept separate "by means of signposts, wire netting, and a uniformed inspector." With their guards down, Flaubert lamented, the "bathing beauties" were anything but:

The human race must indeed have become completely moronic to have lost all sense of elegance to this degree. Nothing is more pitiful than these bags in which women encase their bodies, and these oilcloth caps! What faces! And how they walk! Such feet! Red, scrawny, covered with corns and bunions, deformed by shoes, long as shuttles or wide as washerwomen's paddles.

Dumas, author of *The Three Musketeers* and *The Count of Monte Cristo* and an acquaintance of Flaubert's, started coming in the 1820s, and soon began writing about Trouville. Dumas met for meals with artists Mozin, Isabey, and Huet at what was then called ❻ **L'Auberge du Bras d'Or, 12 rue Charles Mozin.**

Dumas, enchanted with the area's rustic beauty, stuffed himself with locally caught shrimp and sole and invited his Parisian friends to come join in the bounty. With help from the writers and artists, the ancient fishing village gradually took on glamour as the nineteenth century progressed, especially after train service started in 1863, bringing Parisians to town in five hours rather than two days in a horse-drawn carriage.

The painter Gustave Courbet visited Trouville in the summer and autumn of 1865 and reveled in the vast seascapes. "Twenty five autumn skies—each one more extraordinary and free than the last," he enthused to his patron and friend Alfred Bruyas in 1866.

The new fad of "sea bathing" also brought attention to Trouville, with its wide, sandy beaches. The first advertisement for Trouville as a bathing destination appeared in 1837 in the local paper *Le Pays d'Auge*. The industry of sea bathing, which began in England in the early part of the century, had hit France in the summer of 1824 when the duchess of Berry (the daughter-in-law of Charles X) came to the northern French city of Dieppe. After undressing in a bathing hut, the duchess was carried to the water's edge in a chair by the wives of local fishermen.

When the Flauberts began to visit Trouville, society had not yet discovered the town, although sea bathing was increasingly popular. Under the Second Empire, however, during the years from 1852 to 1870, Dieppe was progressively abandoned by high society in favor of Trouville, which was more protected from harsh northern winds. In 1857, sea bathing was strictly regulated by a municipal decree: the beach was divided in three sections, with those for women and men

LES ROCHES NOIRES

The Hôtel des Roches Noires, built in 1866, attracted writers and artists and is now a beachside apartment building.

separated by a mixed section. Swimmers had to change their clothes in beach huts built by the city.

In 1859, the duke of Morny, Napoléon III's half-brother, built a new city across the Touques River from Trouville and called it Deauville. The posh new town attracted some of Trouville's wealthier residents, but despite some fears, it failed to overshadow the original town. The Deauville-Trouville pair has coexisted peacefully since then, with Deauville attracting a flashier clientele and Trouville retaining some of its fishing village charm and maintaining a more artistic and literary bent.

Trouville Today

As the nineteenth century came to an end, writers and artists continued to make Trouville a regular stop along the Normandy coast. Marcel Proust first

Two Writers at the Beach

Another son of a prominent doctor came to vacation in Trouville at the tail end of the nineteenth century. Marcel Proust first came to the seaside town in 1891, a guest of the Baignères family at the villa des Frémonts. Like Flaubert, Proust was pushed by his doctor father to study law, widely viewed as a more respectable occupation than literature. But he, like Flaubert, had little interest in the law. And like Flaubert, Proust was financially independent but had a chronic illness—in his case, asthma—that would at times force him to lead a quiet life of relative seclusion.

Proust went on to write *Remembrance of Things Past*, an autobiographical novel largely narrated in a stream-of-consciousness style. He also wrote some literary criticism. He admired Victor Hugo and considered Charles Baudelaire the greatest poet of the nineteenth century. His views on Flaubert were more complex.

The most famous of Proust's essays is "A propos de 'style' de Flaubert;" in it, he compares Flaubert's use of grammar and tenses to Kant's revolution in philosophy. Although Proust praised Flaubert for his style, he was less complimentary about his subject matter. "I admire Flaubert greatly, but I don't need to be in agreement with an author's conclusions in order to admire his dialect."

came to stay at a villa that belonged to a friend's parents. He returned in 1893 to stay with his mother at ❼ the Hôtel des Roches Noires, 89 rue du Géneral Leclerc, now a beachside apartment building where French writer Marguerite Duras later had a pied-à-terre.

Today, however, the town seems less like a bohemian, artistic hangout than like a playland for fashionable Parisians. On sunny days, visitors in sunglasses crowd the sidewalk cafés, including the famous Les Vapeurs, to feast on platters piled high with shrimp, oysters, and dozens of other sea creatures, while sipping glasses of wine or cider. The chic city folk stroll the boardwalk and swim in the sea on the rare warm days.

Much of the architecture of the current city dates not from Flaubert's time but from the turn-of-the-century Belle Epoque era, when Proust came to visit. The town comprises two sections: the port, which stretches along the inlet to the Touques River and ends at the impressive and ornate ❽ Trouville Casino, designed by the architect Alphonse Durville in 1912; and Trouville's long, sandy beach, which extends beyond the casino. At the time, the 16,000-square-foot building included the Cures Marines, known today as seawater baths, and a music hall. Renovation work started on the casino in 1927 to expand space for gaming. The casino owners acquired the right to operate slot machines in 1992.

Buildings may have come and gone, but Trouville is still most appreciated for its expanse of fine sand that stretches from the casino eastward. The beach offers sharp contrasts; the water can withdraw for more than a mile at low tide, creating an immense stretch of sand, tide pools, and eddies that leave intricate patterns on the

wet sand, which reflects clouds in the typically fast-moving weather patterns. In hot weather, the sea is still and glassy, but as the tide advances and storms approach, waves pound the shoreline.

Bathing huts, which serve as changing rooms and can be rented by the day, still line the wooden boardwalk, and large, colorful parasols dot the beach on warm days. In the late nineteenth century, regular visitors built massive and ornate villas along the beach with broad windows to take in the dramatic and changing seascape. Marguerite Duras, a regular at Trouville until her death in 1996, described the alignment of villas—

Visitors poured into Trouville in the nineteenth century and built a row of villas in diverse architectural styles that adorn the beachfront.

A Fisherman's Shelter

Shoppers examine the daily catch at Trouville's wooden fish market.

As Trouville changed over the years and grew from sleepy town to sophisticated resort, one activity remained constant: fishing. "The most exciting event of the day was when the fishing boats came in," Flaubert writes in "A Simple Heart." Fishing boats still come to set their anchor along the quay of the Touques River, which rises and falls dramatically with the change in tide. And the city's *poissonnerie*, or fish market, remains a central (and aromatic) focal point for the town's daily activity.

Trouville built its first real fish market in 1843 and added a second one in 1881. With Deauville gaining in popularity after World War I, Trouville mayor Fernand Moureaux decided to fight back. But he wanted to boost the town's appeal without changing its history and character. In 1935, he decided the town needed a new and more picturesque fish market. An architect named Maurice Vincent won the design competition with a plan inspired in part by Honfleur's wooden church, the Eglise Saint-Catherine. Now an official historic monument, ❾ **Criée aux Poissons**, Trouville's fish market, still serves as a sort of "town center," with its glistening displays of sole, salmon, shrimp, and dozens of other fish and crustaceans.

built in a diversity of pseudostyles including alpine chalets, Moorish pavilions, and Norman manors—as an illustration of different styles of cinema.

In 1934, Trouville's newly elected mayor, Fernand Moureaux, decided to renovate some city landmarks to emphasize the town's traditional character over Deauville's stylishness. Deauville still caters to a higher-profile clientele, including American movie stars who arrive each September for an annual film festival. But Trouville, thanks to Moureaux and others who have tried to preserve some of the town's traditions, still draws a steady stream of visitors. While paparazzi comb the streets of Deauville, locals and tourists flock to Trouville's Criée aux Poissons (fish auction building) to eye the day's fresh catch of mussels, shrimp, and flounder.

The Road to Honfleur

If Flaubert remained nostalgic about his youth in Trouville until the end of his life, he held similar feelings for Honfleur, just ten miles to the north on a road that winds along the English Channel. His mother, Anne-Caroline Fleuriot, was orphaned as a child and grew up in a boarding school in the ancient port city. In the spring of 1876, four years after her death, Flaubert traveled to Honfleur to do research for "A Simple Heart." In the story, a simple maid, Félicité, suffers a string of losses in her life and ultimately takes comfort in a pet parrot named Loulou. When Loulou dies, Félicité takes her beloved parrot to be stuffed by an expert in Le Havre. She takes the parrot as far as Honfleur, where she puts it on a ship to Le Havre. As she makes her way along the road, she accidentally blocks the path of an oncoming coach and is struck in the face by the coachman's whip. Bleeding but undeterred, she reaches the crest of the hill and looks down on the port:

> As she came to the top of the hill at Ecquemauville, she saw the lights of Honfleur twinkling in the night like clusters of stars and, beyond them, the sea, stretching dimly into the distance. She was suddenly overcome with a fit of weakness and her wretched childhood, the disappointment of her first love affair, the departure of her nephew and the death of Virginie all came flooding back to her like the waves of an incoming tide, welling up inside her and taking her breath away.

Honfleur rose to prominence as a maritime center in the Hundred Years' War when it was fortified by Charles V, but despite the added protection, the English occupied the town from

1419 to 1450. When they departed, the town celebrated by building a wooden church and belfry they called ❿ the Eglise Sainte-Catherine. (Architects and masons were busy reconstructing the region after the war, so wood was the best alternative to stone.) Construction of the church, the largest wooden church in France, started in 1468 on the north nave; the south nave was built thirty years later. It was the work of carpenters who normally built ships, and its two parallel roofs look much like upturned ships' hulls.

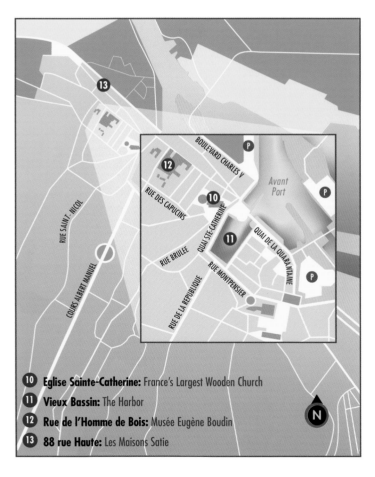

❿ **Eglise Sainte-Catherine:** France's Largest Wooden Church
⓫ **Vieux Bassin:** The Harbor
⓬ **Rue de l'Homme de Bois:** Musée Eugène Boudin
⓭ **88 rue Haute:** Les Maisons Satie

Charles V built fortifications at Honfleur's harbor in order to close the estuary of the Seine from the English. Houses along the Quai Sainte-Catherine are faced with slate and timber.

The old town of Honfleur curves around ❶ the **Vieux Bassin** (old harbor), built under Louis XIV by his chief minister, Jean-Baptiste Colbert. Ship-building flourished here over the centuries, and such famous explorers as Samuel de Champlain—the founder of Quebec—set sail from the port town. Slate-fronted buildings that date from the sixteenth century crowd around the small port, now jammed with sailboats and yachts. The town became a magnet for painters and musicians in the nineteenth century, and the Impressionists held one of their first meetings in a small inn here. Famous natives include Eugène Boudin, born in 1824, and the composer Erik Satie, born in 1866.

Museums dedicated to them—❷ **the Musée Eugène Boudin,** on the **Rue de l'Homme de Bois,** and ❸ **Les Maisons Satie,** at **88 rue Haute**— are now important landmarks.

The Flauberts did not spend a lot of time in Honfleur, but Gustave remained nostalgic about the town because of its importance in his mother's childhood, and also because of the family's close ties with the Le Poittevin family. Alfred Le Poittevin would become one of Flaubert's closest childhood friends. They met because their mothers had been schoolmates and close friends as young girls in Honfleur.

Since then, the well-preserved old city has changed little, although the view across the estuary toward the industrial port of Le Havre provides a sharp contrast to Honfleur's sixteenth-century buildings and winding cobblestone streets that meander up the hill. In 1996, France built a monument to modern engineering that also contrasts with Honfleur's ancient feel. The Pont de Normandie, a bridge connecting Honfleur to Le Havre, was at the time the longest cable-stayed span in the world. Built at the mouth of the Seine, the white bridge stretches 2,800 feet across the estuary and rises 165 feet above the water so as to let ships pass easily underneath.

Honfleur's Eglise Saint-Catherine, the largest wooden church in France, was built by townspeople to show their gratitude at the departure of the English after the Hundred Years' War.

Sailboats line the quays of Honfleur's old port today.

Chapter 4

The Hermit of Croisset

Flaubert's book-lined study at Croisset looked out on the Seine.

The year 1846 had just begun when calamity hit the Flaubert family. On January 15, Dr. Flaubert died at sixty-one following an operation to treat an abscess on his thigh performed by his son, Achille. Six days later, Flaubert's younger sister gave birth to a daughter, also named Caroline. But the young mother soon showed signs of the postpartum infection puerperal fever, which was widespread but poorly understood at the time. (A year later, the Viennese physician Ignaz Philipp Semmelweis determined that the infection was transmitted to women in childbirth by doctors who failed to wash their hands after autopsies and between examinations.) Caroline lingered for two months but died on March 21. Flaubert, his mother, and his infant niece then left Rouen to set up house at their country home in Croisset, leaving brother Achille to live at the hospital apartment with his wife.

It turned out to be a definitive move. Croisset, a country village on the banks of the Seine, wasn't far from Rouen, and Flaubert and his mother often shuttled back and forth between the city and the riverside refuge. But the deaths in the family and the move to Croisset marked a clear turning point in Flaubert's life and career. Finally, he would become what he had always wanted to be: a writer, exclusively. At twenty-five, Flaubert had abandoned his legal studies to devote himself to literature. It had been two years since his first attack of epilepsy, and the frequency of the spells had started to diminish.

By moving with his mother and infant niece to Croisset, Flaubert was choosing both to help his family and to serve as a surrogate father to the baby girl. (Her father, an old schoolmate of his named Emile Hamard, sank into a depression after his young wife's death, and the Flauberts deemed him unfit to take care of her.) To a larger extent, however, the move allowed the writer to excuse himself from a conventional life. Instead of marrying, as had his childhood friends Ernest Chevalier and Alfred Le Poittevin, Flaubert would remain ever faithful to his mother and his work. From then on, despite travels to the Middle East and frequent excursions around France, he would always return to Croisset.

A Gift from a Father

In August 1843, Dr. Flaubert decided to sell the family's country house in Déville-lès-Rouen, which they had

Flaubert spent most of his life and wrote his great books at his family's riverside home.

purchased the year Flaubert was born. The sale was spurred by the railroad's decision to build tracks through the property. In May 1844, Dr. Flaubert bought a new retreat at Croisset, a village made up of a cluster of houses several miles downstream from Rouen, just around the first bend in the Seine. The white, two-story eighteenth-century house there—which looked out at a group of islands in the river and across at the green Normandy meadows—would be Flaubert's principal home for the rest of his life.

After journeying to Italy with his family to accompany his sister, Caroline, on her honeymoon, Flaubert returned to his "cave" at the Croisset house, comparing himself to a bear in hibernation. "Back in my cave!" he wrote to Alfred Le Poittevin in June 1845. "By dint of being in a bad way, I'm in a good way. I shan't be wanting any change in my circumstances for a long time."

From 1851 until his death in 1880, Flaubert's life and the inspiration for much of his work revolved around his close relatives in the region and the house at Croisset. His office was on the second floor of the house, in the western corner. The vast room had five large windows, three looking out on the Seine and two on the garden. Hundreds of books lined the walls,

A rare portrait of Flaubert from the mid-1800s.

and a great bearskin covered part of the floor.

Flaubert often wrote at night, burning candles into the early-morning hours and looking out his windows on the Seine. "The sky is clear, the moon is shining," he wrote to Louise Colet at midnight on an August night in 1846. "I hear sailors singing as they raise anchor, preparing to leave with the incoming tide. No clouds, no wind. The river is white under the moon, black in the shadows. Moths are playing around my candles, and the scent of the night comes to me through my open windows."

Flaubert wrote all of his great works in this room —*Madame Bovary, Salammbô, Sentimental Education, The Temptation of Saint Anthony, Three Tales,* and *Bouvard and Pécuchet*—often laboring through the night, the lamp in his window serving as a beacon to the river boatmen. In the midst of his writing he would roam about, reading his work out loud and even yelling to find the right rhythm and cadence.

A Refuge from the World

Flaubert took an interest in the political upheaval of the post-Napoleonic era—especially the republican insurrection in Paris in 1848—but generally preferred

1848: A Tumultuous Backdrop

On February 23, 1848, Gustave Flaubert and Louis Bouilhet took the train from Rouen to Paris to catch a glimpse of history. Neither was particularly politically minded, but they wanted to see the action, even if only for a brief time. What they saw would change the course of French history and reverberate across Europe. Over the course of twenty-four hours they dined with their friend Maxime Du Camp and wandered through demonstrations that became increasingly bloody and would later be known as the February Revolution of 1848. The street battles pitted Louis-Philippe and his prime minister, François Guizot—who both opposed change—against radicals who wanted universal suffrage and liberals asking for a broadening of voting rights.

On February 24, Louis-Philippe abdicated and fled to England. Turmoil ensued in Paris, with Socialists claiming power and the formation of a Constituent Assembly. By June, class wars were raging in Paris. Thousands were killed or wounded. By this time, however, Flaubert was safely back in Croisset. The bloody skirmishes in Paris did not reflect the general mood in the provinces, where radicals were few. Rouen and other cities were not immune to riots, however. Just two months after the February uprising, an angry mob attacked Rouen's city hall and then battled police for a day before the army quieted the protesters.

The disorder led to a coup d'état two years later, with Louis Napoléon Bonaparte, a nephew of Napoléon, proclaiming himself emperor of France. Napoléon III ruled for the next eighteen years, during what is known as France's Second Empire, a period of industrialization and rapid material progress. Paris in 1848 made a mark on Flaubert even though he watched from the sidelines, and he described the unrest in important scenes in *Sentimental Education*.

He did not feel that he could rely on his recollections alone, however. To re-create the details of the street fighting in February and June 1848, he consulted with friends, including George Sand, and read dozens of books on the subject.

The novel's main character, Frédéric, finds himself near the center of the February street demonstrations, just as he is waiting to meet his beloved Madame Arnoux, the older woman whose character was based on Elisa Schlesinger. "The crowd was growing steadily when all of a sudden the strains of the *Marseillaise* filled the air. It was the column of students arriving. They were marching slowly, in two lines, and in good order. They were not carrying any arms, but they looked angry, and they shouted at intervals: 'Reform for ever! Down with Guizot!'"

Frédéric, like Flaubert himself at that time, was a political bystander, more involved in his own personal relationships, concerns, and work than in the battles that raged in the streets of Paris.

Parisians storm the Tuileries on February 24, 1848.

From Croisset to the Middle East

In October 1849, Flaubert set off for the great voyage of his life. His friend Alfred Le Poittevin had died, and his relationship with Louise Colet had ended (at least for the moment). His mother balked at the idea at first, but Flaubert's brother, a doctor, persuaded her that a trip to warmer climates would be good for her younger son's health. Flaubert and his friend Maxime Du Camp set sail from Marseille for Egypt, where they would begin a two-year journey through the Middle East, including Cairo, the Nile, Jerusalem, Damascus, Constantinople, and finally Greece.

The trip to the Orient was an eye-opening, enthralling experience for a boy from provincial France. Flaubert and Du Camp explored ruins, meandered through ancient capitals, hobnobbed with artists, and cavorted with prostitutes, catching various venereal *chancres* along the way. Flaubert took it all in, observing the exotic new world before him and writing copiously about his experiences to Louis Bouilhet. He also read and reread the classics, and found himself overwhelmed by how much he had not yet mastered. "The man who

In 1849, Maxime Du Camp convinced Flaubert to take off with him on a two-year trip to the Middle East.

retains the same self-esteem while traveling that he had when he looked at himself every day in the mirror of his room at home is either a very great man or a very sturdy fool. I don't know why but I am becoming very humble."

In April 1851, Flaubert and Du Camp made their way to Rome, where Flaubert reunited with his mother. Madame Flaubert wanted him to return quickly to Croisset, so they spent only a few days in Venice. "My mother . . . claims that I've changed and that I have become brutal," Flaubert wrote in his journal. "Which I am not aware of, though I often feel that I'm holding myself back." After Flaubert struck a customs officer in Venice and narrowly escaped arrest, his mother succeeded in hurrying him home to Paris and then Croisset.

to view the tumult from a distance and most often took refuge at Croisset. His friends and literary confidants came to visit often, but when they departed he was left with the solitude he craved. Writing to his mother from Constantinople in 1850, Flaubert explains his reasons for remaining single. The artist, he reasons, is a "monstrosity," living "outside nature." "So (and this is my conclusion) I am resigned to living as I have lived: alone, with my throng of great men as my only cronies—a bear, with my bear-rug as company. I care nothing for the world, for the future, for what people will say, for any kind of establishment, or even for literary renown, which in the past I used to lie awake

so many nights dreaming about. That is what I am like; such is my character."

Flaubert went through periods of seclusion during which he would see few friends and devote himself entirely to his work. He had a fascination with hermits dating back to his childhood, when at the age of ten he wrote to his best friend, Ernest Chevalier, about their visit to what he called Hermit's Rock, an unidentified rock formation located near Port-Mort, a town thirty-five miles southeast of Rouen. As an adult he cultivated the hermit image, although he often entertained his friends and sought companionship in

Rouen and Paris. In a letter to Louis Bouilhet in 1854, while in the midst of writing *Madame Bovary*, he wrote: "I've just passed a week alone like a hermit and calm as a god."

Later in his life he brought his closest friends to Croisset, including the writer George Sand, who wrote of her first visit there, "We got to Croisset at half-past three. Flaubert's mother is a charming old lady. A quiet place; the house comfortable, pretty and well arranged. Good servants; clean; plenty of water; every need thoughtfully provided for. I'm in clover."

Flaubert also used his riverside manor as a refuge from the parts of his life that were incompatible with his mother and his life as a solitary artist. The prime example of this was his refusal to allow his longtime lover, Louise Colet, to come to Croisset and meet his *maman*.

And though he spent some time in Paris during the last decades of his life, he inevitably returned to Croisset. The only exception to this was in 1870, when victorious Prussian troops took over the home for a period of months, sending Flaubert and his mother to stay in Rouen. The troops were gone by July 1871, however, and the two were able to move back home, where they were relieved to find little damage from the soldiers' stay.

The village of Croisset near the Flaubert family's home.

Small steamboats served as river taxis along the Seine dock in Croisset.

Welcome Friends

Many of Flaubert's literary friends came to stay at Croisset, including the following:

Louis Bouilhet: Bouilhet, who was Flaubert's closest male friend during much of the time he lived at Croisset, often came for Sunday dinner. At other times he would sit with Flaubert until the wee hours, listening to him read his latest work aloud. "Bouilhet was here Friday night, Saturday and yesterday morning. He will come again on Wednesday and for the rest of the week," Flaubert wrote to Louise Colet on January 2, 1854. Flaubert called Bouilhet his "literary midwife."

Alfred Le Poittevin: The son of Madame Flaubert's close childhood friend, Le Poittevin was a friend of Gustave's from an early age. He was five years older than Flaubert, who worshipped him and was crushed when he died of tuberculosis in 1848. Le Poittevin came to Croisset during the summer of 1845.

Alfred Le Poittevin was Gustave's good friend and boyhood idol.

Maxime Du Camp: A law school friend, Du Camp encouraged Flaubert to leave Croisset to travel around the Middle East. Du Camp came to visit the writer at Croisset on several occasions. In the summer of 1845 he spent three weeks there, marveling at the beauty of the Normandy countryside and listening to Flaubert read his latest writings.

George Sand: The writer and free spirit gave Flaubert support and sympathy during his later years. The deep friendship between the younger Flaubert and the older Sand was developed mostly in the hundreds of letters they wrote to one another, but Sand also came to visit her friend in Croisset on several occasions, starting in August 1866. She returned in November of that year and wrote in her diary, "After breakfast we went for a walk. I made Gustave come with me; very heroic of him. He got dressed and took me to Canteleu; it's only a short distance away, up the coast. What a lovely landscape, what a pleasant, broad, magnificent view."

Ivan Turgenev: Flaubert met the Russian writer in 1868 in Paris, and the two quickly struck up a warm friendship. Most of their meetings took place in Paris, but Turgenev did venture to Croisset in October 1872, spending several days there listening to Flaubert recite *The Temptation of Saint Anthony*.

Edmond de Goncourt: The Goncourt brothers—Edmond and Jules—were world travelers and writers who collaborated on a series of novels and nonfiction pieces. Edmond came to Croisset in March 1880 with Emile Zola and a small group of other writer friends. It was to be Flaubert's last such celebration.

An Unwelcome Visitor

In June 1851, the writer Louise Colet—Flaubert's longtime lover and one of the century's Romantic literary muses—made an unwelcome visit to Croisset. Unable to reach Flaubert and determined to find him, she took a train from Paris to Rouen, where she booked a room in a hotel and hired a riverboat to take her downstream to Croisset. She arrived in front of the white house in the evening and asked an employee to take a note to Monsieur Flaubert. The maid returned with the following message: "It is impossible for Monsieur to see Madame here."

Flaubert never did allow Colet to come into his home. During the eight years that he carried on an on-again, off-again relationship with the poet and journalist, he remained firm in his edict that she stay away from Croisset and his mother. But from his home office, he would write letter after letter to Colet proclaiming his affection for her and expanding upon his theories of art and literature. She was clearly a difficult person with a stormy personality, but Flaubert's letters to her reveal the depth of their affection.

At the start of their liaison, they would rendezvous for amorous weekends in Paris, and later would meet regularly at a cheap hotel in the city of Mantes, halfway between Paris and Rouen on the rail line. "O bed! If you could speak," Colet wrote in a poem at the time. Yet in the end, these erratic trysts and epistolary outpourings were not enough to satisfy Colet. She wanted commitment—and possibly a baby—from the writer who was famously wedded to his work.

Louise Colet.

A renowned beauty with blond ringlets and an angelic face, Louise Revoil was born in 1810 in Aix-en-Provence, the youngest daughter of a businessman and his aristocratic wife. She showed a talent for poetry as a child, but she was shunned by her siblings after the death of her parents and left the south for Paris as a young bride. She settled in the French capital with her husband, Hippolyte Colet, an assistant professor at the Conservatory of Music. Louise wanted to make an entry into literary society and soon became the lover of the celebrated writer and philosopher Victor Cousin, who helped her win prizes and gain acceptance and some renown in Parisian literary salons.

Louise became more famous when she attempted to stab the well-known columnist Alphonse Karr with a kitchen knife after he suggested in a newspaper column that the baby she was carrying was the result of her liaison with Cousin. Heavily pregnant, Colet surprised Karr in his entryway, but her knife only grazed him. Karr publicized the event, even keeping the weapon on display in his house with the following label: "A gift from Louise Colet—delivered in the back."

Flaubert first met Colet, eleven years his senior, well after her violent outburst, while visiting the Paris salon of the sculptor James Pradier. In July 1846, Flaubert brought Pradier the death mask of his sister, Caroline, so that the sculptor could carve a bust, just as he had done for Dr. Flaubert. This time Colet was there, posing for Pradier. At the time she had been quarreling with Cousin, and her husband was ill with a lung ailment. Flaubert, just twenty-six years old, was a handsome but still unpublished provincial writer. The two quickly began an intense romance that started with a carriage ride through the Bois de Boulogne. After spending several days and nights with his new love, Flaubert retreated to his work and Croisset.

Colet's daughter, Henriette, kept Flaubert's letters to her mother, but almost all of the letters from Colet to Flaubert were destroyed. The writer Francine du Plessix Gray, in her biography of Colet, *Rage and Fire*, hypothesizes that Flaubert himself burned the letters one evening with Guy de Maupassant—a fitting finale to a fiery love affair. Early on in the relationship, Flaubert suggested to Colet—even as he wrote her passionate love letters—that their affair was doomed. A month after meeting her, he wrote, "You think that you will love me for ever, child! What presumption on human lips! You have loved before, have you not? So have I. Remember that you have said 'for ever' before. . . . No matter: I should rather inject some disquiet into your happiness now than deliberately exaggerate its extent, as men always do, to make you suffer the more when it ends—who knows?"

As it turned out, the affair did end badly. And even with their relationship in its death throes, Colet tried once again to visit Flaubert, this time at a flat he was renting in Paris. Breaking off the relationship, Flaubert wrote the following letter to her in March 1855:

> Madame:
>
> I was told that you took the trouble to come here to see me three times last evening. I was not in. And, fearing lest persistence expose you to humiliation, I am bound by the rules of politeness to warn you that I shall never be in.
>
> Yours, G.F.

There Goes the Neighborhood

When the Flaubert's bought their country home, Croisset was little more than a cluster of houses along the Seine. The small village was technically a *hameau*, or neighborhood, of Canteleu, a slightly larger village up the hill looking out on the Seine. The Flauberts' house originally belonged to monks at the nearby Abbey of Saint-Ouen. It had also been the workplace of several noted writers, Flaubert believed. Although details are sketchy, Flaubert told his friends that the writer Blaise Pascal had stayed there and that Antoine-François Prévost, better known as the Abbé Prévost, wrote the first version of his novel *Manon Lescaut* there in the early eighteenth century.

The village of Croisset consisted of a small collection of businesses and a stopping point for the steamers that traveled regularly down the Seine toward Le Havre and the ocean. The larger commune of Canteleu dates back to the Middle Ages, but its name comes from the Latin *cantus lupi* (song of the wolf), and artifacts from Gallo-Roman times have been found in the nearby forests. Evidence of Neanderthal man has also been found in the area, but the tools found were likely from nomadic groups of people. For centuries, however, Canteleu was a typical Norman village known for little more than its magnificent view. In his short story "The Gamekeeper," Guy de Maupassant writes:

> As I went up the hill at Canteleu, I looked over the broad valley of the Seine, the river winding in and out along its course as far as the eye could see. To the right the towers of Rouen stood out against the sky, and to the left the landscape was bounded by the distant slopes covered with trees.

Fast-forward a hundred years, and Flaubert's Croisset has been all but wiped away. The pastoral stretch along

73

Manon Lescaut

Flaubert believed that he was not the first writer to compose literary masterpieces at the stately white house in Croisset. Antoine-François Prévost was trained as a monk in the Benedictine order, but grew weary of the monastic lifestyle and became a traveler and adventurer. Although the dates are not clear, at some point he stopped off at Croisset, Flaubert believed, to work on what would become a classic of world literature: *The Story of the Chevalier Des Grieux and Manon Lescaut*, better known as simply *Manon Lescaut*.

The novel tells the tale of a passionate love affair between a young chevalier, Des Grieux, and a beauty named Manon who is ultimately destroyed by her frivolity. The tragic love story is now better known as the subject of two operas: *Manon,* by Jules Massenet, first performed in Paris in January 1884, and *Manon Lescaut,* by Giacomo Puccini, first seen in Turin in February 1893.

the river evolved into a barren industrial zone after Flaubert's death, while Canteleu spread outward with the building of housing projects after World War II. The writer who despised industry and was profoundly skeptical about his era's faith in "progress" would surely have shuddered if he had seen Croisset's future. His large white house was torn down and replaced by a distillery and then a paper factory, now abandoned.

In the early twentieth century, Rouen's industrial port expanded to Croisset, wiping out any country charm or greenery with its massive steel warehouses and bleak expanses of concrete and industrial waste. The forlorn site now looks like any industrial port, with massive ships passing through and the riverbanks turned into a concrete and metal wasteland.

Croisset's decline as a leafy country getaway mirrors the port of Rouen's shift toward oil and gas in the late

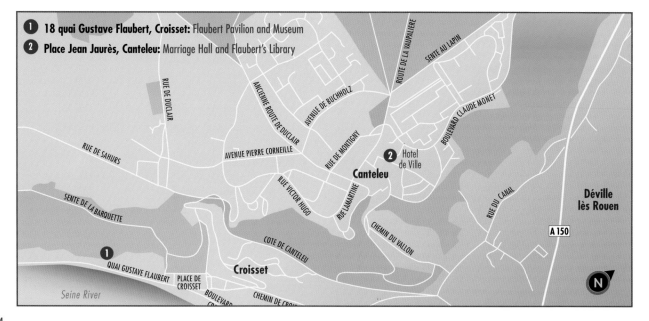

1 **18 quai Gustave Flaubert, Croisset:** Flaubert Pavilion and Museum
2 **Place Jean Jaurès, Canteleu:** Marriage Hall and Flaubert's Library

Flaubert's pavilion now looks out across a busy road to the industrial port of Rouen.

Flaubert's "Linden Alley" today. Flaubert would pace back and forth between the lindens while shouting out his newly composed sentences.

nineteenth century. From the fifteenth to the eighteenth centuries, the region's shipowners and navigators had forged trade relations all around the world. During the same year that Flaubert moved definitively to Croisset, the port of Rouen got a boost from city fathers, who passed a law on May 31, 1846, allowing the river and estuary to be widened, making room for the largest ships to sail to Rouen. In the twentieth century, the petroleum industry flourished and Rouen became a major transfer point for bulk shipments of oil, phosphates, wood products, and wine. The city also built oil refineries, and heavy industry spread up the Seine to Croisset and beyond.

For today's visitor seeking traces of Flaubert, only the garden pavilion remains. In the small pavilion, which the Flauberts called the *petit salon*, Flaubert would sometimes retreat to receive guests or watch the Seine flow by in the moonlight. The pathway leading from the pavilion to the house was bordered by a row of

linden (sometimes called lime) trees. Flaubert called it his *gueuloir* (shouting ground), and he would pace back and forth there, reading and shouting his sentences to test their rhythm and cadence.

❶ **The Flaubert Pavilion and Museum, 18 quai Gustave Flaubert**, is now a small museum in what is now called Dieppedale-Croisset. Owned and run by the city of Rouen, it is a sad sight, sitting alone amid Rouen's industrial port. Instead of meadows and a large tulip tree, the solitary building is surrounded by stretches of grey concrete. Many of the writer's personal possessions are on display: portraits, busts, photographs by Nadar, an armchair, the famous stuffed parrot that Flaubert may or may not have used for inspiration while writing the story "A Simple Heart," an inkwell, goose quills, and a writing case. If Flaubert felt that

writers and artists should leave little behind but their words, he succeeded in this case.

A Writer's Life

Flaubert's daily routine at Croisset revolved around his family and his work. According to his niece Caroline's *Souvenirs Intimes (Intimate Memories)*, written in 1926,

The pavilion at Croisset is all that remains of Flaubert's home.

Flaubert's mother doted on him, having little social life of her own. Flaubert typically rose at 10 a.m., read his letters and the newspaper, dressed, and performed his *toilette*, just in time to go down to lunch with his mother and niece and the occasional visitor. After lunch, he smoked his pipe and strolled outside in the garden and along the Seine until the boat from Rouen to La Bouille, near the mouth of the Seine, whistled by. Then it was time for Caroline's lessons. The two would head for his study, where Caroline liked to stretch out on his bearskin rug as her learned uncle told her tales of ancient Greece and Rome. As the years passed the lessons would become more complicated, and when Caroline turned ten Flaubert had her start taking notes during his lessons on history, literature, and geography.

This idyllic life came to a crashing halt seven years later. At the age of seventeen, Caroline developed a crush on a young artist who was giving her painting lessons. Flaubert and his mother disapproved of this man with no fortune or prospects, and quickly arranged a marriage in 1864 with Ernest Commanville, a successful thirty-year-old lumber importer. Caroline was miserable, but after the exhortations of her uncle, she consented. The two stayed together until Commanville's death in 1890, although Caroline was never happy in the marriage. She said early on that she never wanted to have children, and the couple did not produce any offspring.

Flaubert helped to raise and educate his niece, Caroline, but then encouraged her to marry a man she didn't love.

Ironically, Flaubert's early enthusiasm for Commanville would come to haunt him in his later years. His mother, who died in 1872, left the Croisset property to Caroline, with the stipulation that Flaubert could stay there until his death. Caroline—perhaps at the urging of her husband—started criticizing her uncle for careless housekeeping, calling him "the consumer." Flaubert had given his money to Commanville to manage, so he was forced to beg for his own money from Caroline.

In the mid-1870s, in the years following Madame Flaubert's death, the lumber industry suffered and Commanville faced financial ruin. To save the Commanvilles from bankruptcy, Flaubert agreed to sell his only property—a farm in Deauville that was his chief source of income. Despite the conflict and financial hardship, Flaubert remained devoted to his niece, perhaps remembering that he had played a part in urging her to marry Commanville even as she had sobbed and protested.

Death and Destruction

In the end, Flaubert's home—the house where he had spent most of his life—did not belong to him. To make matters worse, he feared that he might eventually have to leave the house if Commanville could not solve his deepening financial problems. That did not happen, but in the year following Flaubert's death, Commanville did sell the house to pay off his own debts. The demolition began in August of that same year. "They cut down the apple trees that make this bit of Normandy so typical of Normandy," the newspaper *Le Figaro* reported at the time. "In less than a month everything was gone: the entrance gate with its porch and its lime trees where you waited for the boat to Rouen, the tall railings where you used to see Flaubert

Ernest Commanville, a thirty-year-old lumber importer, seemed to Flaubert and his mother like a good match for the teenage Caroline.

walking, the cluster of trees where he used to sit in the summer."

Caroline Commanville, unhappy in her marriage, was clearly distraught by the sale, although she saw no alternative. "With only a few day's notice I had to leave all my childhood memories behind me," she wrote to family friend Edma Roger des Genettes in June 1881. "And what was even dearer to me—those connected with my beloved uncle, and this seemed to me like a second death."

A Library Lives On

After Commanville's death, Caroline worked with a group of friends to buy back the pavilion in order to preserve a small remnant of her uncle's life in Croisset. A small museum was opened there in 1906. Caroline kept Flaubert's most important possessions, however, including his manuscripts and library. After she remarried, she took them with her to the southern Mediterranean town of Antibes, where she lived until her death in 1931 at the age of eighty-four. She donated the original manuscripts to Rouen's library, and toward the end of her life she entrusted her collection of Flaubert's library furniture and books to a neighbor, the writer Louis Bertrand. In 1936, Bertrand in turn donated the collection to the Académie Française in exchange for a payment of 9,000 francs.

When Bertrand died in 1941, the books were put into storage in the south of France and then were taken to an Antibes museum for safekeeping in August 1944 for fear they might

Getting Out: Parisian Gatherings

While Flaubert was known as "the hermit of Croisset" and liked to cultivate an image as a solitary writer, the title was not always accurate. As he aged, he developed a taste for fashionable Parisian literary salons, especially after he began a friendship with Princesse Mathilde Bonaparte, the flamboyant cousin of Napoléon III. In 1862, at the age of forty-two, he began attending the Magny dinners, which were started by the influential literary critic Charles Saint-Beuve. In a private dining room at the Restaurant Magny on the Rue Mazet in the Latin Quarter, Flaubert wined and dined with fellow literary stars, including Jules and Edmond Goncourt and the Russian writer Ivan Turgenev, who would become a close friend.

Over the next few years, the Magny dinners brought Flaubert in contact with a wide circle of literary friends. The most important friendship of his later years was with George Sand. He had begun corresponding with her in 1863, but it was not until 1866, at Magny's, that the pair finally met in person. Sand wrote in her diary about her first Magny dinner, noting "Flaubert, impassioned and more sympathetic to me than the others. Why? I'm still not sure." She was more critical of some other participants: "There is a superabundance of paradox and self-esteem." And she seemed less than enthralled by the mostly masculine banter: "Everyone pays 10 francs, the dinner is mediocre. There's a lot of smoking and loud talk; and you leave when you like." Sand would return regularly to the dinners, however, and would attend more frequently than Flaubert, who was often plagued by boils and sometimes found it difficult to leave Croisset.

The dining room of Mathilde Bonaparte, in her mansion on the Rue de Courcelles in Paris, where Flaubert often attended Wednesday evening soirees.

be damaged in Allied bombing raids. In 1949, the Académie—with which Flaubert had not always been on good terms—donated the library to the Association of Friends of Flaubert and de Maupassant.

The town of Canteleu, with help from Rouen-based Flaubert scholar Edmond Ledoux, eventually inherited Flaubert's collection. In July 1952, a truck traveled from Antibes to Croisset to drop off the twenty-three cases of books and furniture. Flaubert's library was restored and set up for display in the main room of the town hall, within walking distance of the pavilion.

The roughly eight hundred books, which include an 1837 edition of Cervantes's *Don Quixote*, Shakespeare's plays, and dedications from Victor Hugo, came primarily from the library of Flaubert's father, who gave his scientific and medical books to Flaubert's brother, Achille. It is clear from examining his favorite tomes that Flaubert treated his books with reverence. He rarely wrote on the pages, but left traces of pencil in the margins to mark his favorite passages.

In 1990, the town hall moved into modern offices up on the plateau of Canteleu, where ❷ **Flaubert's library** is now set up in the *salle des mariages* (marriage hall) at **Place Jean Jaurès**. Visitors can view the collection if they make an appointment with town administrators. Thus, while Flaubert's home and office are long gone, his beloved books have been carefully restored and remain in their original bookcases only miles from Croisset.

The Académie Française

The Académie Française serves as a sort of moderator of the French language, determining standards of correct grammar and vocabulary. It regularly elects esteemed writers to serve as members, although Flaubert was never invited to join.

The Académie was born in the 1630s when a group of literary men met to discuss language, rhetoric, and criticism. In 1635, Cardinal Richelieu officially recognized the organization, which has since then (except for the period between 1789 and 1803) considered itself the overseer of French language and literature. Members have helped prepare and revise a dictionary, and in the nineteenth century the body started to distribute grants and awards for "courage" and "civic virtue."

Critics have charged the Académie with having excessively conservative views on literature. Flaubert never considered membership a worthy goal—he regularly made fun of it with his friends, although Maxime Du Camp was made a member in 1880. Flaubert was not alone in remaining outside the Académie; the elite organization has shunned a number of illustrious writers over the years, including Molière, Jean-Jacques Rousseau, Honoré de Balzac, Emile Zola, and Marcel Proust.

Chapter 5
Ry and Lyons-la-Forêt
The Land of Emma Bovary

Ry's main street, where the real-life Madame Bovary was said to have lived, cuts a straight line through the town.

L'H., Paris

The small town of Ry sits quietly in a modest river valley, surrounded by farmland and cow pastures. Only ten miles northeast of Rouen's bustling center, Ry moves at the slow pace of rural life. Tractors lumber through the town center, and locals gather to chat and smoke at a sidewalk café. At first glance, this unremarkable town of 618 inhabitants has nothing to distinguish it from the rural villages that dot the Norman countryside.

Upon closer investigation, however, clues to Ry's claim to fame start to pop up. First, there is the graphic image of a woman's face that appears on road signs. The face, with two crescents of dark hair, heart-shaped lips, and eyes glancing seductively to the side, is meant to represent Emma Bovary, Flaubert's most famous heroine, and is now a kind of local trademark. The names of local businesses also give it away: Video Bovary, Le Grenier Bovary (antiques), La Rotisserie Bovary, Le Jardin d'Emma (flowers).

Shortly after the publication of *Madame Bovary* in 1856, experts and locals started to draw parallels between Ry and Flaubert's fictional town, Yonville-l'Abbaye. Even today, Flaubert's rough sketch of Yonville, with its long main street (called the Grande Rue), bears a resemblance to Ry.

Man and dog gaze out a window on Ry's main street.

fifteen miles south of Ry. Still, literary legend has been hard to kill. While Flaubert scholars consider the "land of Emma Bovary" cultivated by Ry's town fathers to be a sort of Disneyland filled with half-truths and misconceptions, curious visitors continue to make the pilgrimage to the town that considers itself the home of the real-life Emma Bovary.

Finding Emma

The face that now adorns road signs for miles around Ry serves as a constant reminder to passersby of Emma's tragic fate. Although Flaubert denied it, *Madame Bovary* was almost certainly inspired by *un fait divers* (a news item), the story of Delphine and Eugène Delamare, who lived and died in the small town of Ry. Delphine Couturier was the second wife of Eugène Delamare, who had been a medical student of Flaubert's father in Rouen. Eugène had never passed all of his exams, however, and so became an *officier de santé*, a sort of second-tier medical practitioner. Delphine, the daughter of a local farmer, quickly grew to despise her husband, according to legend, and proceeded to take lovers and spend lavishly on fancy clothing and extravagant curtains. The story has been embellished over the years, and the finer details are hard to pin down; some Flaubert biographers claim that she was beautiful, while other say she was plump and pale but with a seductive walk.

From the start, however, Flaubert denied the connection. "I used no model," he wrote soon after the book was published. "*Madame Bovary* is pure invention." And over the years, filmmakers have preferred the more picturesque town of Lyons-la-Forêt,

Though the exact details of her life are disputed, the memory of Delphine Delamare lives on in modern-day Ry. Just several feet from the door of the town's church, a yellow tombstone confirms that she died in 1848 at the age of twenty-six. Carved beneath her name on this stone, purchased by the town to replace the old one in 1990, are the words "Madame Bovary." Like Emma Bovary, Delphine—in despair over her mounting debt and loveless marriage—poisoned herself, the story goes. Her husband, like Charles Bovary, died soon after, leaving a young orphaned daughter and a story that refused to fade away.

The Flaubert family knew the Delamares, and Flaubert most likely knew of Ry. Delamare had been a student of Dr. Flaubert's, and Madame Flaubert, according to one report, had helped the young couple by lending them three hundred francs. Despite these family connections—or perhaps because of them—Flaubert was initially reluctant to tell this story. His friend Louis Bouilhet urged him on, however, and in September 1851 he began the four-and-a-half-year process of writing Madame Bovary. "Last night I began my novel," he wrote to Louise Colet. "Now I foresee difficulties of style, and they terrify me."

Soon after his pen hit paper, he cast Louise Colet as his epistolary confidante with regard to Madame Bovary. And if Delphine Delamare and Ry first inspired the story, the actual characters and sites seem more likely to be amalgams of several towns and women. As he developed the character of Emma, he read the types of romantic books that appealed to girls at the time and questioned Colet about her own youth. "For two days now I have been trying to enter into the dreams of young girls, and for this have been navigating in the milky oceans of books about castles, and troubadours in white-plumed velvet hats. You can give me exact details I need," he wrote to Louise in March 1852.

Louise, who along with Louis Bouilhet helped Flaubert through the difficulties and loneliness of writing Madame Bovary, was also a model in certain ways for the character of Emma. Like Emma, Louise had acquired her first taste of literature and romance from second-rate novels. And like Emma, Louise was famously narcissistic and often dissatisfied with her lack of riches and her less than brilliant husband. Details in the novel also point to Louise. Most notably, the motto amor nel cor (everlasting love), which is inscribed in the ring that Emma gives to her lover, Rodolphe, had been—in real life—etched on the cigar holder Louise gave to Gustave at the start of their affair.

Louise Colet wasn't the only Louise who served as model for Emma, however. Louise Pradier was the wife of James Pradier, a much older man and the most successful sculptor of the day. Flaubert had taken the death masks of his father and his sister to Pradier so that he could sculpt busts. Unlike Emma, Louise Pradier lived in luxurious quarters and presided over a salon

Delphine Delamare's tombstone. Was she the real Emma Bovary?

What Does Emma Bovary Look Like?

Flaubert disliked illustrations of his work, so there is no early engraving or drawing of his most famous character. Rarely has such a character, variously adored and reviled by so many, been so hard to picture. From Flaubert's description, we know she had dark hair parted in the middle and brown eyes that sometimes appeared to be black. The signs that surround Ry show Emma with two smooth rolls of black hair on either side of her face and eyes cast to the side. A portrait of a young woman painted by the Rouen artist Joseph-Désiré Court adorns some recent editions of *Madame Bovary*. Court's painting depicts a sad-eyed young woman engaged in some kind of needlework, but with eyes looking to the side.

Flaubert liked to describe parts of Emma, but despite his realist style, he never offered a full picture of his character. When Charles Bovary first meets her, he is "surprised by the whiteness of her fingernails. They were almond-shaped, tapering, as polished and shining as Dieppe ivories. Her hands, however, were not pretty—not pale enough, perhaps a little rough at the knuckles; and they were too long, without softness of line." He then focuses on her eyes. "They were brown, but seemed black under the long eyelashes; and she had an open gaze that met yours with fearless candor."

Later, early in their marriage, Charles describes the joy he feels when observing his new wife: "In bed in the morning, his head beside hers on the pillow, he would watch the sunlight on the downy gold of her cheeks, half covered by the scalloped tabs of her nightcap." Again, he examines her eyes. "Seen from so close, her eyes appeared larger than life, especially when she opened and shut her eyelids several times on awakening; black when looked at in shadow, dark blue in bright light; they seemed to contain layer upon layer of color, thicker and cloudier beneath, lighter and more transparent toward the lustrous surface."

This 1844 portrait by Joseph Court has often been used to depict Emma Bovary.

that brought together great poets, artists, and a collection of the city's most fashionable residents.

But like Emma, Louise was not easily satisfied, and she was eventually brought down by a combination of promiscuity and debt. Her husband grew tired of her stream of lovers and extravagant ways, and cast her off. Flaubert himself was reportedly one of her lovers, and while writing *Madame Bovary* he borrowed from her unpublished memoirs, underlining passages and making notes in the margins.

Writing *Madame Bovary*

Flaubert was thirty years old and still unpublished in France when he shut himself in his Croisset office to write his great novel. In France, it was a time of change. King Louis-Philippe had recently abdicated and fled to England. Prince Louis Napoléon Bonaparte was elected president, and in 1851 he declared himself president for life. Within a year, he named himself

Emperor Napoléon III. So began the Second Empire in France, a period of industrial expansion and urbanization. Railways crisscrossed Normandy and other regions of France. Baron Haussman rebuilt Paris with vast boulevards lined with ornate stone buildings, and Rouen and other major cities followed suit.

During this time of economic growth and industrial progress, Flaubert was focused on exposing the hypocrisies of small-town, middle-class society. He progressed slowly—five hundred words a week. During this time, however, he was also writing copiously to Louise Colet, expanding on the joys and pains of artistic creation. "It is splendid to be a great writer, to put men into the frying pan of your words and make them pop like chestnuts," he wrote in November 1851. "There must be a delirious pride in the feeling that you are bringing the full weight of your ideas to bear on mankind. But for that you must have something to say. Now, I will confess to you it seems to me I have nothing that everyone else doesn't have, or that hasn't been said equally well, or that can't be said better."

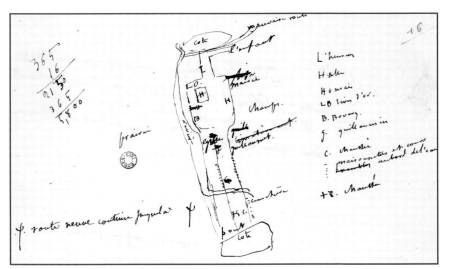

As Flaubert made progress he gained confidence, although he experienced mood swings that left him alternately in despair and jubilant. Increasingly, he was pouring himself into his character, experiencing all of her emotional and even erotic euphoria. On December 23, 1853, he reached the high point. Emma and Rodolphe become lovers in a scene that takes place in a forest on an autumn

Flaubert's sketch of Yonville shows his vision of the small Normandy town.

afternoon. "Since two o'clock yesterday afternoon (except for about twenty-five minutes for dinner), I have been writing *Bovary*," he wrote to Louise Colet on a Friday night at 2 a.m.

> *I am in full fornication, in the very midst of it: my lovers are sweating and gasping. This has been one of the rare days of my life passed completely in illusion, from beginning to end. At six o'clock tonight, as I was writing the word 'hysterics,' I was so swept away, was bellowing so loudly and feeling so deeply what my little Bovary was going through, that I was afraid of having hysterics myself.*

By 1855, Flaubert had finished two-thirds of his novel, had spilled out thousands of words on the process to Colet, and was ready to break off their relationship. Near the time that he wrote his final letter to Colet, he was describing in his book how the gentleman farmer Rodolphe Boulanger broke off his affair by dashing off a brief note to Emma, who was expecting him to run away with her. After composing the letter, Rodolphe showed little emotion, "smoked three pipes and went to bed."

Flaubert struggled to complete *Madame Bovary*. As he complained to Louis Bouilhet in September 1855, "My wretched novel won't be finished before February. This is becoming ridiculous. I don't dare mention it any more." By April of that year, he had finished the manuscript. His old friend Maxime Du Camp—who was then the publisher of a literary review, the *Revue de Paris*—agreed to print *Madame Bovary* in serial form. Fearing that the novel's scenes of adultery would shock some, Du Camp suggested cutting certain sections, but Flaubert protested. In the end, the two agreed to cut one scene—Emma's cab ride through the streets of Rouen with her lover, Léon.

From the first installment's publication, *Madame Bovary* caused a stir, drawing protests by readers outraged at the book's "immorality." Then the government stepped in, and Napoléon III's censors asked the Department of Justice to prosecute the magazine and Flaubert for "outrage of public morals and religion." Even as Flaubert signed a contract with the publisher Michel Lévy to have his work published in book form, the government continued with its legal case. In January 1857, Flaubert wrote to his brother Achille: "At any moment, I expect the summons that will name the day when I am to sit—for the crime of writing in French—on the bench usually occupied by pick-pockets and prostitutes."

Flaubert went to trial that same month. Maître Jules Sénard, a prominent trial lawyer who had been a friend of Dr. Flaubert's, defended him. In a four-hour presentation, Sénard described the Flaubert family's stature and Gustave Flaubert's education and impeccable upbringing. He went on to defend *Madame Bovary* as a useful portrayal of the middle class and a condemnation of hypocrisy in society, not a glorification of adultery. Sénard's speech was considered a triumph, and Flaubert was acquitted on February 7.

Flaubert's trial most likely helped make *Madame Bovary* a success while turning its author into a public figure for the first time. The first six thousand copies sold quickly, and there were two more printings during the course of 1857. Reviews, however, were not all glowing. In Rouen, Flaubert was considered an eccentric, and even the most respected literary critics in Paris found the book too pessimistic, especially in its final chapters. Charles Saint-Beuve, perhaps the most influential critic of his time, praised the early scenes of small-town Normandy life, but criticized the cruel ending, which he complained lacked signs of human goodness. In the end, however, he acknowledged Flaubert's talent,

Flaubert's Lawyer

Maître Antoine-Marie-Jules Sénard was no ordinary lawyer. Sénard, born in 1880, had been a friend of Flaubert's father and was not only a distinguished legal figure but also a powerful political force in France. A committed republican, Sénard would go on to serve as a minister of the interior and a diplomat late in his career. In January 1856, Sénard had already established himself as a prominent trial lawyer who had played a role in the organization of meetings that led to the February Revolution of 1848. In particular, he had participated in an important "reform banquet" held in Rouen just before the revolution. Such reform banquets were political meetings in disguise, which allowed those in favor of political change, and of wider voting rights in particular, to gather.

While Flaubert did not share Sénard's fervor for political reform or oratory, he would come to appreciate the man who staked his own reputation on defending him. On January 29, 1857, in a courtroom at Paris's imposing Palais de Justice, Sénard rose to make his case for *Madame Bovary*, Flaubert, and literature. Responding to the state prosecutor, Ernest Pinard, who had warned that *Madame Bovary* would negatively influence young girls and married women because Emma is never effectively condemned in the novel, Sénard started out by providing a brief family history of the Flauberts. Once he had established the family as well respected and highly educated, he went on to describe Flaubert's writing style and explain that *Madame Bovary* was not a glorification of adultery, but rather a study of real characters and real life that produces "a useful result."

The next day, Flaubert wrote to his brother, Achille: "Maitre Sénard's speech was splendid. He crushed the attorney from the Ministry of Justice, who writhed in his seat and made no real rebuttal." A week later, the court acquitted Flaubert. Writing to friends just after the decision, he proclaimed himself physically and emotionally exhausted.

Maître Jules Sénard, a prominent lawyer and friend of the family, defended Flaubert and *Madame Bovary*.

When Madame Bovary was subsequently published, Flaubert dedicated the book to his defender, writing:

Antoine-Marie-Jules Sénard
Member of the Paris Bar, Ex-President of the National Assembly and Former Minister of the Interior

Dear and Illustrious Friend,
Permit me to inscribe your name at the head of this book, and above its dedication; for it is to you, before all, that I owe its publication. Reading over your magnificent defense, my work has taken on for me an unexpected authority. Please accept the homage of my gratitude, which, however great it is, will never attain the height of your eloquence and your devotion.

Gustave Flaubert
Paris, April 12, 1857

proclaiming, "The son and the brother of eminent doctors, Gustave Flaubert wields the pen like a scalpel."

Battle of the Towns

Despite clues to the contrary, Flaubert never admitted publicly that *Madame Bovary* was based on his own acquaintances or on a true story, one that took place so close to his home in Rouen. When cross-examined about Emma's identity, he famously claimed, "*Madame Bovary, c'est moi*" ("I am Madame Bovary"). This puzzling and somewhat misleading reply reflects his identification with a character who could not bear the contrast between her romantic dreams and the dull routine of her life. He also maintained that Emma was everywoman. In his writings after *Madame Bovary* was published, Flaubert spoke of his novel as a universal tale. "My poor Bovary, no doubt, suffers and cries in 20 French villages at this very moment," he wrote to Louise Colet in August 1853.

Ry, and a few other towns, didn't buy this explanation. Advocates for Ry were the first to make their case. In 1907, a Dr. R. Brunon wrote in *La Normandie Médicale* (*Medical Normandy*) that another doctor in Rouen had told him twenty-eight years before about the story of Delphine Delamare. All of the details were interesting, the doctor wrote, and "show more clearly than all of the critics how Flaubert was the inventor of the documentary—not the realist—novel."

For decades, however, other amateur critics have had their say. In 1957, one such observer proclaimed, in a fierce polemic published by the Association of Friends of Flaubert and de Maupassant, "Yonville-l'Abbaye is not Ry!" In the same year, another critic launched a counterattack, insisting *"Ry ou rien"* (Ry or nothing), in an article entitled "In the Land of Emma Bovary." Still,

Gustavus Flaubertus, Bourgeoisophobus

In December 1852, Flaubert wrote to his friend Louis Bouilhet to thank him for some Latin verses. In the midst of writing *Madame Bovary*, Flaubert took a break from the seriousness of his work to write a playful letter using the sixteenth-century spelling of one of his favorite writers, Michel de Montaigne. In keeping with the mocking tone, he signed the letter in Latin: Gustavus Flaubertus, Bourgeoisophobus.

For much of his life, Flaubert was full of scorn for his century's increasingly prosperous class of merchants, doctors, lawyers, and other professionals. (Even though his own father and brother were well-known doctors, Flaubert sometimes criticized the profession in his work.) His fictional town of Yonville was a microcosm of the values of bourgeoisie society—or, worse still, of the society of the *aspiring* bourgeoisie. Emma herself is continually caught up in buying clothes and fancy home furnishings in her attempt to escape her misery. She is then tormented by the sinister merchant Monsieur Lheureux, who plays on her weakness for luxury only to turn on her. The hapless Charles Bovary attempts an experimental operation to fix a clubfoot only to have the operation fail and the patient lose his leg. In the end, the pompous town pharmacist Monsieur Homais triumphs, as do the bourgeois values that Flaubert so detested. "The devil himself doesn't have a greater following than the pharmacist: the authorities treat him considerately, and public opinion is on his side," the novel concludes. "He has just been awarded the cross of the Legion of Honor."

a seed of uncertainty had been planted. Could the real Yonville be, in fact, another town in this region of upper Normandy? Advocates for the nearby Forges-les-Eaux, Neufchâtel-en-Bray, and Lyons-la-Forêt have in turn argued that Flaubert's Yonville more closely resembles their communities. Filmmakers Jean Renoir and Claude Chabrol both chose Lyons-la-Forêt as the setting for their versions of *Madame Bovary*.

Ry's Victory

Modern critics believe that Flaubert's Yonville probably existed in the writer's imagination, or was at least an amalgam, like the character of Emma herself. "Let's not say: Ry or Forges? But rather Ry and Forges," suggested J. Pommier, a professor at the Sorbonne, in an article in 2004. Ry appears to have won the battle, however, because its inhabitants care more. Unlike Forges-les-Eaux, a spa resort known for its iron-rich waters, or Lyons-la-Forêt, a beautiful town of half-timbered houses located in a forest where the dukes of Normandy once hunted, Ry is undistinguished and plain. No famous writers or artists were born there, and its history can be reduced to a paragraph. So even though the Yonville described by Flaubert is filled with prudes and hypocrites, Ry clings to this distinction.

Unlike its competitors, Ry rarely appears in guidebooks or history books outside of references to its association with Flaubert, although settlement in the town and its surrounding area dates back to Roman times. The

Cows graze on a farm near Ry.

fifty local parishes, all linked to Rouen. Above all, the region has been for centuries a center of agriculture and an important marketplace for grain and produce.

Ry sits in what is now called the "three valleys," an area that includes villages, farms and châteaux, and two other small rivers, the Andelle and the Héronchelles. This northeastern slice of upper Normandy is known as the Pays de Bray, or Bray region. It is bordered on the east by the Picardy region and on the west by the flatter Caux region, a chalk plateau that stretches to the ocean. Throughout the region, farmland is peppered with well-preserved monuments such as the Château de Martainville, built in the fifteenth century, and ruins such as those at Le Héron, a château originally built in the seventeenth century and the site of a party attended by Flaubert when he was a teenager.

The town of Ry is still little more than that single road, "long as a rifle shot," described by Flaubert. The town's church, ❶ the Eglise Saint-Sulpice, perches on a slope to the north, looking down on one end of the main street. The church, built in the twelfth and thirteenth centuries, has been classified as a historic monument because of its wooden porch, an intricately sculpted Italian-style entryway that was made in the sixteenth century and tacked onto the older structure. Centuries later, the Delamares were laid to rest beside it.

The Crevon River flows through the town of Ry.

town's name comes from the Latin *rivus* (small river) or from the Gallic *ritum* (stream), according to local historians, a reference to the town's location on the Crevon River. From the thirteenth century until the French Revolution, the town was the seat of a group of

The Château de Martainville, built of brick in 1485, now houses a museum displaying Normandy art, furniture, and traditional objects.

A Stroll through Town

Local tourism officials, seeking to capitalize further on the Bovary connection to their region, have put together a thirty-seven-mile excursion that they call a "promenade in the land of Emma Bovary," which includes houses and landmarks that may have appeared in the novel. The "Emma Bovary Circuit," leaving from Ry, takes the visitor through the small towns and farmland in the valley of the Crevon, Héronchelles, and Andelle rivers. At each of fifteen sites, a large sign explains the significance of the village or monument. Some, such as Ry, are clearly tied to Flaubert.

Le Héron

At the age of sixteen, Flaubert was invited to a lavish reception in a château at Le Héron. Some say this experience inspired his description of Emma's visit to La Vaubyessard, where she is delighted and awed by the slice of upper-class life. "Then, late in September, something exceptional happened: she was invited to La Vaubyessard, home of the marquis d'Andervilliers." When she returns after the party to her modest home and quiet existence as a country doctor's wife, Emma is deeply disappointed and increasingly dissatisfied with her life. "How remote the ball already was! What was it that made tonight seem so very far removed from the day before yesterday? Her visit to La Vaubyessard had opened a breach in her life, like one of those great crevasses that a storm can tear across the face of a mountain in the course of a single night."

The château at Le Héron was destroyed after World War II, but an unusual funeral chapel remains in the middle of the woods near the remains. The 1868 structure was built in a neo-Byzantine style, an uncommon sight in the region.

This funeral chapel, built in 1868, sits in the woods near the site of the château at Le Héron.

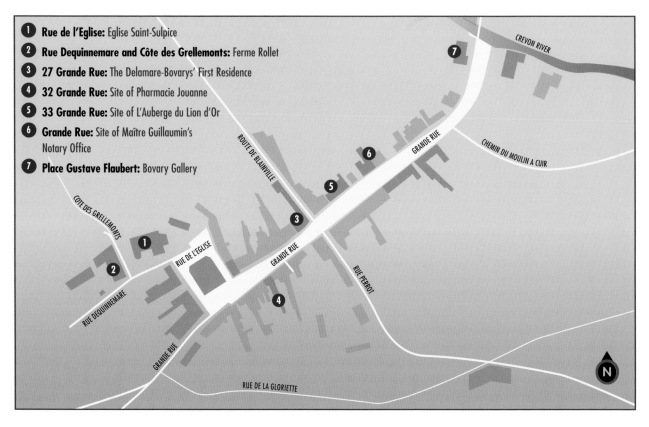

1 **Rue de l'Eglise:** Eglise Saint-Sulpice

2 **Rue Dequinnemare and Côte des Grellemonts:** Ferme Rollet

3 **27 Grande Rue:** The Delamare-Bovarys' First Residence

4 **32 Grande Rue:** Site of Pharmacie Jouanne

5 **33 Grande Rue:** Site of L'Auberge du Lion d'Or

6 **Grande Rue:** Site of Maître Guillaumin's Notary Office

7 **Place Gustave Flaubert:** Bovary Gallery

Others are just interesting stops on the tour. The first site encountered is ❷ **the Ferme Rollet**, now thought to be a renovated farm not far from the church. In the novel, Emma takes her infant daughter there to stay with a wet nurse. When hit with a sudden urge to visit her baby, she makes her way toward the house, "at the end of the village at the foot of the hills, between the main road and the meadows." Though the farm is not far from the center of town, the trip is arduous for the new mother. On her way, she meets Léon, the clerk who later becomes her lover. "To reach the wet nurse's house they had to turn left at the end of the village street, as though going to the cemetery, and follow a narrow path that led them past cottages and yards between privet hedges."

A stroll down the Rue de l'Eglise leads to the Grande Rue (main street), now a part of the departmental D13 road, which includes several stores and businesses named after Emma Bovary. When asked if Ry is the real Yonville, an employee at Ry's tourism office responds, "Of course!" Local tourist guides provide a list of addresses for sites that appear in the novel: ❸ **Emma and Charles's first residence**, which had a door onto an alleyway that allowed Emma to come and go without being seen, is now a notary's office; the old

❹ **Pharmacie Jouanne,** which existed in 1850 and is now a hardware shop, is thought to be the Pharmacie Homais so carefully described in the novel:

But what catches the eye the most is across the square from the Lion d'Or hotel: Monsieur Homais' pharmacy! Especially at night, when his lamp is lit, and the red and green glass jars decorating his window cast the glow of their two colors far out across the roadway! Peering through it, as through the glare of Bengal lights, one can catch a glimpse, at that hour, of the dim figure of the pharmacist himself, bent over his desk.

Construction of Ry's church began in the twelfth century, but a sculpted wooden porch was added in the sixteenth century.

The *Madam Bovary* tour continues down the Grande Rue. ❺ **The Auberge du Lion d'Or** is now a bank rather than a hotel. ❻ **The notary office of Maître Guillaumin,** the lawyer who turns down Emma's plea for financial help near the novel's end, is now part of a store called La Rêve Ry.

At the end of the main street, an old cider pressoir (cider-making house) has been transformed into the village's main tourist attraction. ❼ **The Bovary Gallery,** on the **Place Gustave Flaubert,** boasts a collection of five hundred animated puppets, three hundred of which reenact scenes from *Madame Bovary* during daily performances. The figures are only a few inches tall and move mechanically to background music. The main scenes are all there—Emma dancing at her wedding, Charles sawing off the leg of Hippolyte, Emma and Léon ripping off their clothes. Visitors to the museum can also view a

95

Was this building the original Pharmacie Homais?

reconstruction of the 1850 Pharmacie Jouanne, as well as documents relating to the Delamares.

Emma Goes to Lyons-la-Forêt

Flaubert brought Emma Bovary to life with his pen, but he never wanted to see his work performed on stage. After his death, however, he couldn't stop the productions—both theatrical and cinematic—that followed. Over the years, filmmakers have made nine adaptations, with various levels of success.

Two of those filmmakers, Jean Renoir in 1933 and Claude Chabrol in 1991, chose the town of Lyons-la-Forêt over Ry and the other contenders for their setting. Both Renoir and Chabrol made heavy use of the town's picturesque central square to reconstruct the important market scenes. Chabrol literally transformed the town by removing cars and television antennae and bringing in hundreds of actors and actresses dressed in period costume. "Flaubert had a cinematographic mind," Chabrol told a writer for the *Telegraph* newspaper in 1991. "I am sure that he would have hurled himself on a movie camera if it had existed in his time."

Chabrol's version, which was praised by Flaubert scholars but received mixed reviews from film critics, is faithful to the text, although Chabrol focused even more than did Flaubert on the character of Emma, portrayed with intensity by the French film star Isabelle Huppert. Although Huppert's face dominates the screen for much of the movie, Lyons-la-Forêt also plays a starring role, with its rows of half-timbered houses and surrounding forest of beech trees.

Lyons-la-Forêt is picture-postcard beautiful, and it knows it. Flowers of every color spill from meticulously maintained hanging pots that rim the road and decorate the central town square. The town, filled with charming restaurants, hotels, and antique shops, feels more like a posh weekend getaway spot for Parisians

than the ordinary town that Flaubert describes in *Madame Bovary*. That's not surprising, given its past brush with royalty.

The town is nestled amid La Forêt Domaniale de Lyons, thousands of acres of predominantly beech forest twenty-one miles from Rouen and ten miles south of Ry. The town's history goes back to Gallo-Roman times (some remnants from that era have been discovered at the site). In the twelfth century, the duke of Normandy had a residence here—Henry I, William the Conqueror's fourth son, who was known as Henry Beauclerc, built a fortress on what is now the town's center. Henry died of food poisoning in this château in

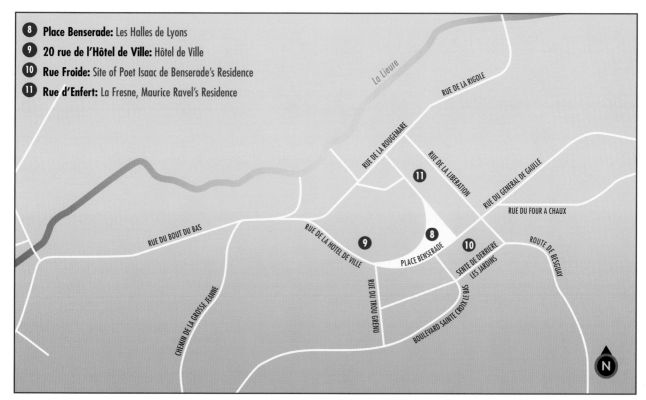

8 **Place Benserade:** Les Halles de Lyons

9 **20 rue de l'Hôtel de Ville:** Hôtel de Ville

10 **Rue Froide:** Site of Poet Isaac de Benserade's Residence

11 **Rue d'Enfert:** La Fresne, Maurice Ravel's Residence

1134. According to legend, he died just after eating lamprey eels and taking part in a hunting expedition in the nearby forest. (Henry was known for his love of the lamprey, a long, scaleless river fish which looks like an eel but is a parasite that attaches itself to other fish. Lampreys were particularly popular in England, where the fish was considered a delicacy at court.)

In the center of town, ❽ **Les Halles de Lyons**, a marketplace in the **Place Benserade**, dates from the eighteenth century in its current form after being restored by the duke of Penthièvre. Claude Chabrol made further improvements to the wooden, thatched-roof market structure before filming much of *Madame Bovary* in the town's center. The marketplace still attracts local farmers several mornings a week, when shoppers peruse baskets of fruit and vegetables and rows of fresh eggs and local cheeses.

Among the well-preserved buildings in town, Lyons-la-Forêt's ❾ **Hôtel de Ville** (town hall), **20 rue de l'Hôtel de Ville,** has been classified a historic monument by the French government because it was built on the foundation of Henry I's château. The current structure was built in the eighteenth century and still boasts many of its original furnishings.

Flowers adorn the center of Lyons-la-Forêt.

Local farmers sell their wares at Lyons-la-Forêt's marketplace, which Claude Chabrol restored before filming *Madame Bovary* there in the early 1990s.

The Dukes of Normandy

Driving on the narrow roads that make their way through the Lyons forest, it is easy to picture the hunting parties that once chased deer and wild boar through the tangle of beech trees. The roads and even the châteaux are new since the dukes came to frolic, but the forest itself remains mostly untouched.

The dukes of Normandy, who ruled parts of France and England for hundreds of years, claimed a title held by various Norman, French, and English rulers from the tenth century, when the Viking leader Rollo took charge in 911.

In 1066, perhaps the best known of the dukes, William the Conqueror, added the kingdom of England to his domain through the Norman Conquest. The Bayeux Tapestry—an embroidery more than 230 feet long and 20 inches wide—now hangs in the Normandy town of Bayeux (125 miles to the west of Lyons-la-Forêt) and tells the story of the Norman invasion of England. The tapestry, which was believed to have been commissioned by Bishop Odo, the bishop of Bayeux and the half-brother of William the Conqueror, is made up of hundreds of images that allow the viewer to "read" the story from start to finish.

The story is told from the Norman perspective and focuses on the story of William, who before his victory was known as William the Bastard because he was born illegitimate after his father, Robert the Magnificent, had an affair with a tanner's daughter.

The Norman dukes ruled during a time of prolonged struggle between lands and people on both sides of the English Channel. They brought to England a centralized form of feudalism, which had been developed in Normandy, in which king and people, lord and vassal, were bound in a sort of contract. This new model contrasted sharply with that of the all-powerful Roman emperor.

After William, English kings continued to claim the title of duke until the Treaty of Paris in 1259. English monarchs tried to reclaim their Norman possessions during the Hundred Years' War, but were ultimately left with only the Channel Islands, a part of the duchy since 933, which they still hold today.

William the Conqueror, who was also a duke of Normandy, is seen in the eleventh-century Bayeux Tapestry, which tells the story of the Norman invasion of England.

The town prides itself on its artistic residents. The poet Isaac de Benserade, for instance, was born here in 1612. ⑩ **Benserade's residence** was near the central town square, on the **Rue Froide**. He was a favorite in the courts of Louis XIII and Louis XIV, and was called upon to write libretti for royal ballets. Before making his name in the courts, Benserade wrote a series of sonnets, including "On Job" in 1651, which unleashed a court debate over poetic style. Two centuries later, the musician Maurice Ravel came to stay at a house called ⑪ **La Fresne,** on the **Rue d'Enfert.**

Today, however, Lyons-la-Forêt's biggest attraction is the forest that surrounds it. Once a favored hunting ground for royalty, the forest covers 26,440 acres and is now filled with winding roads and hiking trails. Several small villages, châteaux, and abbeys are also sprinkled through the forest, which is France's largest beech grove.

Built in the seventeenth century, the stately Château de Vascoeuil was home for twenty years to the nineteenth-century French historian Jules Michelet, who wrote his multivolume *History of France* there (at roughly the same time that Flaubert was writing his novels at Croisset). The château is now a museum open to visitors.

A Garden Where Sculptures Grow

The region that cultivates its ties with Flaubert was also the stomping ground of another great Rouen writer's family. An expansive park and stately château called Bois-Guilbert was built just before the French Revolution. The property was once held by the family of the seventeenth-century dramatist Pierre Corneille, a native of Rouen known for his tragedies, including *Le Cid*.

A young sculptor named Jean-Marc de Pas, himself a descendant of Corneille, inherited the property and has transformed it into a garden filled with contemporary sculpture that includes many of his own works as well as those of friends. Located in the small farming town also called Bois-Guilbert—twelve miles north of Ry—the château and garden provide a sharp contrast to the surrounding agricultural landscape. Giant ants made of steel appear to march across a vast lawn; a bronze form of a woman reclines on a chair; bronze figures embrace in the middle of a field.

Sculptor Jean-Marc de Pas inherited the Bois-Guilbert château and has turned the grounds into a vast sculpture garden.

Chapter 6

Pont-l'Evêque

"Thus it is with all our dreams"

B y the time he had reached his early fifties, Flaubert considered himself an old man, and the feeling was reinforced by a quick succession of deaths among his close friends. The rush toward the grave began in 1869, when Louis Bouilhet died at the age of forty-eight after a brief illness. Another close friend, Jules Duplan, succumbed several months later in March 1870, followed by Jules de Goncourt, who died of syphilis in June. "Eight days ago I made a sad trip to Paris—what a funeral!" he wrote to his niece, Caroline. And to his friend Edmond de Goncourt (the brother of Jules), he repined: "So I live alone with my mother, who grows older every day, and more feeble, and complaining. A conversation of any serious kind has become impossible with her, and I have no one to talk to."

The period of gloom would only darken when victorious Prussian soldiers marched into Normandy later that year, ultimately evicting Flaubert from his home for a period of several months. After the troops had left, he returned home to Croisset in March 1871. Then, in 1872, Flaubert's mother died, leaving Croisset to her niece with the stipulation that Flaubert could live there until he died. In the next few years, his money troubles mounted while his literary reputation came under assault. *The Temptation of Saint*

View of Pont-l'Evêque's Eglise Saint-Michel.

The center of Pont-l'Evêque was heavily bombed in World War II and has since been rebuilt.

Franco-Prussian War

In July 1870, France declared war on Prussia. Napoléon III started the war on what could be considered trivial grounds—the refusal of Prussia's royal house to renounce its ambitions to take over the Spanish throne. The declaration turned out to be an unwise move for France, whose army was no match for Prussia, which had come to dominate a loose federation of German territories. Flaubert voiced his own disapproval to George Sand, writing on August 3, "I feel we are entering black darkness." Soon, however, alarmed by reports from the battlefront, Flaubert turned patriotic, proclaiming that the Empire must be defended "to the end."

The end, as it turned out, was not far off. The Prussian army mobilized, quickly took over large parts of France, and soon defeated the French army at the battle of Sedan, where Napoléon III was taken prisoner on September 4, 1870. In December, Prussian soldiers marched into Croisset—and into Flaubert's home—forcing him and his mother to take up temporary residence in Rouen.

Flaubert was horrified when the Prussian army marched into Paris on March 1, and he pictured the scene even though he was not there. "All day I saw the bayonets of the Prussians flashing in the sun on the Champs-Elysées, and heard their bands playing under the Arc de Triomphe!" he wrote to Princess Mathilde from Rouen. "The man who sleeps in the Invalides must have turned in his tomb today."

In the period that followed, a revolutionary state known as the Paris Commune came into power and engaged in a bloody civil war that shook all of France. The Commune lasted from March to May 1871, ending when the forces of the National Assembly quashed the revolutionary forces, laying the groundwork for France's Third Republic.

Even as the battles raged in Paris, Flaubert was trying to put the war and subsequent disruption behind him. "Contrary to my expectations, I find myself very well off at Croisset," he wrote to Caroline on April 4, 1871. "I think no more about the Prussians than if they had never come here! It was a very sweet feeling to be back in my study and see all my little belongings again."

Napoléon III surrendering.

Anthony was published in 1874 to largely negative reviews, and his one attempt at playwriting, *The Candidate*, was jeered off the Paris stage after a single performance. His latest project, a novel about two clerks called *Bouvard and Pécuchet*, was not going well.

A Bath of Memories

With help from his surviving friends, most importantly George Sand and Ivan Turgenev, Flaubert struggled to keep writing. It was Sand who—seeing that her younger friend was suffering as some critics dismissed

his work as too negative—advised him to "write something more down to earth that everybody can enjoy." Flaubert took her advice and returned to the landscape of his early childhood. In April 1876, he traveled to his mother's hometown of Pont-l'Evêque to complete the research for what would be one of his most celebrated pieces of work, "A Simple Heart." The trip, a fifty-three-mile trek from his home in Croisset, sent him on an emotional journey that rekindled his earliest memories but also reminded him that his life was nearing its end. "This excursion plunged me into melancholy, for inevitably it was a bath of memories," Flaubert wrote to his friend Edma Roger des Genettes. "How old I am, *mon Dieu*! How old!"

Notwithstanding such melancholy, while writing "A Simple Heart" Flaubert experienced a happiness he had rarely known and would never feel again. In the warm summer heat, he swam in the Seine and wrote happily into the evening. "Before dinner, around seven, I frolic in the bourgeois waters of the Seine," he told Guy de Maupassant. And to his niece he wrote, "In the night the sentences go rolling through my mind like the chariots of some Roman emperor, and they wake me with a start by their jolting and their endless rumbling."

Sand, in the last months of her battle against cancer, had finally succeeded in cheering up her gloomy friend.

Light after Darkness

Flaubert grouped "A Simple Heart" with two other short stories to form *Three Tales*, which was published in 1877. ("The Legend of Saint Julian the Hospitator" was inspired by a stained glass window in Rouen's

Russian writer Ivan Turgenev, a dear friend, kept in close touch with Flaubert and urged him to continue writing.

An Unlikely Alliance

Gustave Flaubert and George Sand formed an unlikely pair. When they began their friendship and correspondence, Sand was fifty-eight and an established novelist, while Flaubert was a forty-one-year-old bachelor, increasingly shut off from society in his book-lined study.

Born Amandine-Aurore-Lucile Dupin in Paris in 1804, Sand lived a turbulent life, punctuated by affairs with famous figures such as the great pianist Frédéric Chopin. In the 1830s she separated from her husband and started to publish her writing in order to earn extra money. Soon she yearned to enter the intellectual life that was traditionally barred to women, so she donned men's trousers and a hat in order to gain entrance to restricted libraries, museums, and other forbidden locales.

By the time she met Flaubert, however, Sand was a grandmother living with her son and his family in Nahant. Back in her skirts but retaining her rebel spirit, she had a generally optimistic view of human nature and was a beloved and prolific writer. Flaubert, by contrast, was unfailingly pessimistic about humankind and worked to keep moral judgments out of his work. And he hadn't always been a fan of Sand's writing. At the age of twenty-seven he had expressed his scorn for Sand's more emotional style, writing in his first version of *Sentimental Education* in 1843, "I do not address these remarks to the schoolboys and dressmakers who read George Sand . . . but to persons of discrimination."

Once the pair started corresponding, however, their differences drew them together. "I don't think there can be two workers in the world more different from one another than we are," Sand wrote. "But as we are so fond of each other it doesn't matter. . . . We need our

George Sand.

opposite number." Over the course of their ten-year correspondence, each served as a sounding board for literary opinions and political points of view, while also providing moral support and comfort during sometimes difficult times.

Flaubert, who at times revealed a certain disdain for women and their literary talents, called Sand "chère maître" (dear master). Sand, who had been forced to take a man's name to gain credibility, called him "my dear old Troubadour." At times they grated on one another, and they rarely changed each other's mind, but the letters kept flowing. Sand visited Flaubert at Croisset several times, while Flaubert made the trip to Nahant on occasion, and the two also met at times in Paris.

When Sand died of cancer in June 1876, Flaubert was devastated. After her death—just ten months before "A Simple Heart" was published to widespread acclaim—he told her son Maurice: "I began A Simple Heart exclusively for her, solely to please her. . . . She died when I was in the middle of my work. Thus it is with all our dreams."

He felt, he confided in Maurice, as if "I was burying my mother for a second time." Flaubert had depended on her, as he had on his mother. And the two women both admonished him at different points for focusing on the written word at the expense of human relationships. Unlike his mother, though, Sand understood his literary aspirations. In a letter to another loyal female correspondent, Marie-Sophie Leroyer de Chantepie, Flaubert wrote: "One had to know her as I did, to realize how much femininity there was in that great man, and the vast tenderness in that genius. Her name will live in unique glory as one of the great figures of France."

cathedral, and the final story, "Herodias," is a reworking of the tale of Salomé and John the Baptist.)

Unlike his earlier novels, the story was universally well received. Some, however, questioned whether the novelist, who so often created characters who were hypocrites and charlatans, was truly sympathetic to his simple-minded, illiterate Félicité. He was, he insisted. The story, he wrote to his friend Edma Roger des Genettes in June 1877,

> is quite simply the tale of the obscure life of a poor country girl, devout but not given to mysticism, devoted in a quiet sober way and soft as newly baked bread. . . . It is in no way ironic (though you might suppose it to be so) but on the contrary very serious and very sad. I want to move my readers to pity, I want to make sensitive souls weep, being one myself.

Calvados and Camembert Country

The backdrop for Flaubert's story is Pont-l'Evêque and the surrounding Pays d'Auge, a region of green hills and dairy farms that stretches from the coastal resort towns of Deauville, Trouville, and Cabourg; inland to Pont-l'Evêque; south to the commercial and industrial town of Lisieux; and beyond to the cheese-producing villages of Livarot and Camembert. The region is quintessential Normandy, with pasturelands, hilly apple orchards, thatched cottages, and manor houses.

The Pays d'Auge, which straddles the departments of Calvados, Orne, and part of the Eure, is best known as the heart of production for some of Normandy's most tasty products: slightly alcoholic sparkling cider; its distilled product, the apple brandy known as calvados; and rich and aromatic cheeses such as Camembert, Pont-l'Evêque, and Livarot. Flaubert, as any good

Norman, was a fan of these local delicacies and compared himself as he aged to a runny Camembert.

This region of lower Normandy, wedged between a plateau that surrounds the city of Caen to the west and the broad, flatter agricultural fields to the east, is made up of gentle hills, hidden valleys, and a countryside that is perhaps the most lush and fertile in Normandy. Local tourism officials, eager to spread the word about their sometimes hidden treasures, have created the "Cider Route," a twenty-five-mile trail that wanders through the picturesque towns of Beuvron-en-Auge, with its rows of half-timbered houses and central square, and past the market towns of Cambremer and Bonnebosq. In between, area farms advertise tastings of cider and calvados.

Maman's Home

Flaubert knew Pont-l'Evêque and the surrounding region well from his childhood visits, and "A Simple Heart" is clearly autobiographical and full of sentiment for the area. It is the tale of a humble and loyal Pont-

l'Evêque maid named Félicité who suffers through a succession of disappointments and heartbreaks, only to find comfort in her pet parrot. The character of Félicité was inspired by the Flaubert family's maid and nanny Julie, who had loved Gustave when he was a child— and who was not only still alive in the 1870s

Madame Flaubert in 1870.

107

The Land of Cheese

Charles de Gaulle once famously inquired, "How can anyone govern a nation that has 246 kinds of cheeses?" Normandy, with its fertile soil and milk-producing cows, is responsible for a major portion of the country's important cheese-making tradition. And three of the country's most famous cow's-milk cheeses—Pont-l'Evêque, Camembert, and Livarot—hail from the Pays d'Auge region, where small farmers still labor to produce them.

Pont-l'Evêque, a square cheese, has been made in Normandy since the twelfth century. It was mentioned in the thirteenth-century novel of courtly love *Le Roman de la Rose*, but was known then as Angelot and served as money to trade against other products. The aromatic cheese took on its current name in the seventeenth century and remains popular today.

The lesser-known Livarot, a round, orange cheese traditionally wrapped in the leaves of a grass known as sedge, comes from a small town south of Pont-l'Evêque. The town of Livarot organizes an annual cheese festival in July, complete with a cheese-eating contest.

Camembert, perhaps France's most famous cheese of all, was born during the French Revolution (so the legend goes), when a farmer named Marie Harel created a round cheese and named it after her small town. Camembert was first packaged in a wooden box and given its famous label at the end of the nineteenth century. It was then sent off to Paris and all over Europe, where it was soon copied.

Small farmers in the towns of Camembert and Pont-l'Evêque still labor to produce the cheeses that have made the area famous.

but vigorous enough to come to visit Flaubert while he was writing the story. (Félicité and Julie were by no means identical, however; Félicité, for instance, is depicted as simple and uneducated, whereas Julie was well read.) The children in the story, Paul and Virginie, were no doubt based on Flaubert and his sister, Caroline, who had died just after giving birth to her daughter many years before.

In the story the Aubain family, which comprises the widowed Madame Aubain and her two children, live in Pont-l'Evêque in a house "with a slate roof" that "stood between an alley and a narrow street leading down to

the river." Flaubert paints a picture of a lonely woman: "A narrow hallway separated the kitchen from the living room in which Madame Aubain remained all day long, sitting in a wicker armchair close to the casement window."

Straddling the Touques River just seven miles from the Trouville beaches, Pont-l'Evêque as a settlement dates back to the Roman period, when roads linking Bayeux and Rouen passed through the area. When a series of bridges over nearby rivers made the voyage easier, merchants settled in the area and Pont-l'Evêque (which means, literally, "bridge of the bishop") was crowned the capital of the Auge region. But the city never built

Pressing the Apples

The apple tree is said to have grown first in the Tien Shen mountains in eastern Kazakstan, but Normandy has adopted the fruit as its own, and apple orchards have covered the landscape for centuries. In addition to slicing the fruit into tarts and adding it to stews, the Normans have been fermenting apples since at least the tenth century, when Vikings drank a beverage known as *bjorr*. In the thirteenth century, pressing and crushing techniques improved and alcoholic cider spread throughout the region.

The apple brandy known as calvados is created from cider in the same manner that cognac is made from wine: through double distillation in copper stills. The brandy, which is 70 percent alcohol, is reduced to a slightly lower strength, aged from three to twenty-five years in oak casks, and then bottled. In 1942, the French government bestowed its coveted Appellation d'Origine Contrôlée (AOC) status on the drink, guaranteeing that true calvados can be made only within the region. (The French initiated the AOC system in 1935 to ensure that wines, cheeses, and other prized food products are made using certain traditions and standards.)

Calvados made within the Pays d'Auge region, considered to be the highest quality, is generally put through a double-distillation copper-pot still, as opposed to the more mechanized single-column still used in other parts of Normandy. Family-run farms still dot the Pays d'Auge, offering tastings of cider, calvados, and pommeau, a mixture of apple juice and calvados.

A copper still and cider-making tools.

walls to protect itself, so it was an easy target for the English forces who invaded and took over in 1346. The English occupied the town again from 1417 to 1449, and then once more in 1490, when Henry VI's army seized the town. Part of the town and its fifteenth-century church, ❶ the Eglise Saint-Michel, were destroyed in the battle, but they were subsequently restored.

Pont-l'Evêque today looks little like the town where Flaubert's mother was born to Anne Charlotte

Cambremer and Jean-Baptiste Fleuriot, a medical officer, in 1793. Roughly 65 percent of the town was leveled by Allied bombing raids at the end of World War II, although the Eglise Saint-Michel and some other buildings have been carefully restored.

The Eglise Saint-Michel figures prominently in "A Simple Heart":

Genuflecting as she went through the door, Félicité walked up the aisle beneath the high ceiling of the nave, opened the door of Madame Aubain's pew,

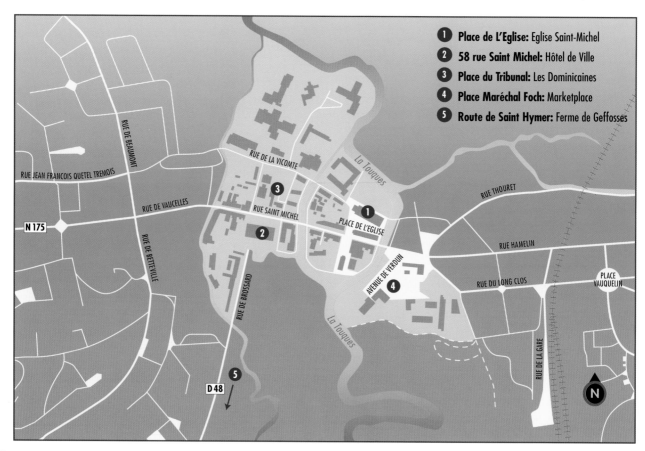

❶ **Place de L'Eglise:** Eglise Saint-Michel
❷ **58 rue Saint Michel:** Hôtel de Ville
❸ **Place du Tribunal:** Les Dominicaines
❹ **Place Maréchal Foch:** Marketplace
❺ **Route de Saint Hymer:** Ferme de Geffosses

sat herself down and looked all around her. The children were seated in the choir stalls, the boys on the right and the girls on the left. The priest stood in front of them beside the lectern. One of the stained glass windows in the apse showed the Holy Spirit looking down on the Virgin Mary. In another, the Virgin knelt before the infant Jesus and behind the tabernacle there was a carving in wood representing Saint Michael slaying the dragon.

Despite the massive destruction at the end of the war, the town has kept some of its charm. Bright flowers spill over railings along the river, which splits into two tributaries at the center of town. Some remnants of the past remain: ❷ **the Hôtel de Ville** sits at the southern entrance to the town in an eighteenth-century building once called the Hôtel de Brilly. It was the birthplace of the late-nineteenth-century writer Robert de Flers, known for dramatic works inspired by his interest—much like Flaubert—in Middle Eastern travels. Across

The Touques River cuts through Pont-l'Evêque.

the street (the Rue Saint-Michel), the city has restored a Dominican convent, ❸ **Les Dominicaines,** built in the fifteenth and sixteenth centuries, which is now a museum and cultural center.

Town life centers on ❹ **the marketplace,** where local farmers bring their wares every Monday for one of the largest and liveliest markets in the region. Under the covered marketplace, shoppers peruse dozens of local cheeses, freshly laid eggs, sausages, prepared rabbits and ducks, and homemade preserves, while fresh fruits and vegetables are piled high on tables just outside. Locals with overflowing baskets jam the aisles, and shoppers come from miles around to stock up on the farm-fresh delicacies.

A Family Farm

Farmers large and small continue to sow the fields, make cheese from local cow and goat milk, and grow apples in the miles of orchards that fill the Pays d'Auge. Flaubert's family owned one such local farm, ❺ **the Ferme de Geffosses,** less than a mile from the center of Pont-l'Evêque. The farm, originally owned by relatives of Madame Flaubert, sat on a rise looking down over gentle rolling hills. In 1746, the twenty-five-acre farm was sold to Pierre Cambremer des Aulnées. Madame Flaubert inherited several parcels from this relative, and Dr. Flaubert bought the rest in 1829 and enlarged the farm by buying adjacent land two years later. Although the land was owned by the Flauberts, a family named Deslandre ran the farm for much of the nineteenth century.

Flaubert visited the farm as a child and describes it in "A Simple Heart": "Whenever the weather was fine, the whole family would get up early and spend the day at the farm at Geffosses. The farmyard there was on a

slope, with the farmhouse in the middle. One could just see the sea, a little streak of grey in the distance."

Flaubert goes on to describe scenes of the brother and sister playing that likely came from his own childhood:

Félicité would take a few slices of cold meat from her basket and they would eat in a room adjoining the dairy. This room was all that now remained of

An old poster advertises the charms of locally made Calvados.

a country house which had fallen into ruin. The paper hung in strips from the wall and fluttered in the draught. Madame Aubain sat with her head bowed, absorbed in her memories, the children hardly daring to speak. "Off you go and play," she would say. And off they went. Paul would climb up into the barn, catch birds, play ducks and drakes on the pond or bang the great farm barrels with a stick to make them boom like drums. Virginie would go and feed the rabbits or run off across the fields gathering cornflowers, showing her dainty embroidered knickers as she ran.

Madame Flaubert left the Geffosses farm to her oldest son, Achille, who sold it the following year, in 1873. The farmhouses, apple orchards, and farmland have been turned into an upscale bed-and-breakfast. Large hedges now obscure the distant view of the ocean, and the farmhouses have been rebuilt and modernized. Ducks and geese still wander the property, however, and the five guest houses have been named after Flaubert's works: "Madame Bovary," "A Simple Heart," "Sentimental Education," "Herodias," and "Salammbô."

The Last Years

By the time Flaubert published his popular *Three Tales*, the financial misfortunes of his niece and nephew had forced him to sell his own farm in nearby Deauville. With Geffosses also sold off, he had no more ties to the region, so once his mother and Sand were gone, he retreated increasingly to Croisset. "The death of our

Flaubert's family owned the local Ferme de Geffosses.

poor Mme. Sand grieved me immensely," Flaubert wrote to Ivan Turgenev in June 1876. "I wept like a calf at her funeral, twice: the first time, when I kissed her granddaughter Aurore (whose eyes, that day, were so like hers as to be a kind of resurrection); and the second, when I saw her coffin carried past me." George Sand's death followed by only three months the death of Flaubert's longtime lover Louise Colet, and the disappearance of two women so important to him hit hard. "My heart is becoming a necropolis," he wrote to Princesse Mathilde.

Sinking again into melancholy but still communicating with the small group of remaining friends and family members, including Guy de Maupassant, Emile Zola, and his niece, Caroline, Flaubert pressed onward with his final novel, *Bouvard and Pécuchet*, which he ultimately left unfinished. The last few years of his life were taken up with worry over the state of his finances, sadness over the loss of friends, and hard work on this last novel, for which he accurately predicted there would be little interest from his reading public. "*Bouvard and Pécuchet* keeps trotting along," he wrote to Guy de Maupassant in August 1878. "I've made almost all of my notes—I've been doing nothing else for the past month—and I hope to begin writing in about a fortnight. What a book! As for expecting that the public will read a work like this—what madness!"

Alone at Croisset in the winter of 1879, Flaubert wrote to his niece about his loneliness and the comfort that his childhood nurse, Julie (who was old and feeble by this time), still provided. "I satisfy my need for affection by calling in Julie for a talk after dinner and looking at the old black-and-white checkered dress that Maman used to wear."

A Last Glimmer before Darkness

In March 1879, Ernest Commanville's sawmill was sold for a fraction of its estimated value. The disastrous sale was the culmination of the financial worries that consumed Flaubert's later years. The money he had fronted the Commanvilles in an attempt to save them would never be repaid. Flaubert now held responsibility for Commanville's remaining debts; payment of those debts had been guaranteed by Flaubert's friends Edmond Laporte and Raoul Duval, and this put a strain on their friendship.

Portrait of Flaubert in his later years.

That same month, however, Flaubert was informed by Guy de Maupassant that he would be offered a pension from the Ministry of Education. "Princes have always given such things to their great men; why shouldn't our government do the same?" wrote de Maupassant to Flaubert. And much to his relief, Flaubert received official word seven months later that the state pension had come through. "I have the honor to inform you that I have decided you should be awarded an annual grant of three thousand francs," wrote France's minister of education, Jules Ferry, on October 3, 1879.

This good news lifted Flaubert's spirits and saved him from financial ruin, although he was soon after devastated by a falling-out with Edmond Laporte, who had guaranteed loans to Commanville. When differences over repayment arose, Flaubert sided with his niece and her husband and, with much sadness, ended the friendship.

A Final Send-Off

After the distressing severing of ties with Laporte, Flaubert sought to reinforce his remaining close friendships as he struggled to reach the end of his last novel. The winter of 1879–80 was a cold one, and early on he started planning a reunion of friends and celebration at Croisset. He invited fellow writers Emile Zola, Georges Charpentier, Alphonse Daudet, Edmond de Goncourt, and his disciple, Guy de Maupassant.

The group of friends arrived at Croisset on Easter Sunday, March 28, 1880. Flaubert welcomed the men at his house, "wearing a broad-brimmed hat and short jacket, with his big behind in pleated trousers, and his kind, affectionate face," Edmond de Goncourt wrote in his journal that day. Goncourt found Croisset more beautiful than he had remembered. "The enormously wide

The writer Emile Zola as painted by Edouard Manet.

115

Seine, with the masts of invisible ships passing by as though against a backdrop in a theater; the splendid tall trees, their shapes tormented by the sea winds; the garden with its espaliers, the long terrace-walk facing full south."

The fellow writers enjoyed a dinner of turbot in cream sauce, drank many kinds of wines, and spent the evening telling bawdy stories, "which had Flaubert shaking with laughter, the laughter of a child's pure mirth."

Flaubert's friends left the next morning, spent the afternoon in Rouen, and took the evening train back to Paris. Alone again at Croisset, Flaubert made plans to travel to Paris. Progress on *Bouvard and Pécuchet* was slow, and he needed a break. "I've got to the point of scarcely knowing what I'm doing," he wrote to Ivan Turgenev on April 7, 1880. "Every bone in my body aches, I have stomach cramps, and I scarcely sleep. But enough moaning."

Flaubert never made it to Paris. On May 8, he rose late, bathed, performed his toilette, and read the morning mail while he waited for breakfast. There, in his family home just a few miles from his birthplace in Rouen, Flaubert died.

The exact circumstances of his death remain unknown, although Caroline wrote in her memoirs that he died of a massive stroke. De Maupassant backs up that account in a letter to Turgenev. Some of his other friends, including de Goncourt, claimed that he died of an epileptic fit, with the telltale foam on his lips.

Flaubert's Legacy

Flaubert's funeral took place three days after his death, and his friends and protégés, including Zola and de Goncourt, dropped their activities to pay a last tribute to him. "The death of Gustave Flaubert hit us all like a lightning bolt," Zola wrote. A group of about two hundred mourners gathered in Croisset, and the cortege wended its way up the hill to Canteleu for a short church service. The mourners then made their way toward the city and to the Cimetière Monumental in Rouen, which sits on a hill looking down on Rouen's rooftops and many church steeples. There, Flaubert would rejoin his parents, his younger sister, and his friend Louis Bouilhet.

The group that followed Flaubert did not grow as it entered Rouen, however. "What is inexplicable,

Fellow writer Edmond de Goncourt admired Flaubert's home and garden at Croisset.

An Unfinished Work

In June 1874, Flaubert set off with friend Edmond Laporte to find the right setting for his final novel, *Bouvard and Pécuchet*. He settled on the region between the cities of Caen and Falaise, on what he called a "stupid plateau." By "stupid," he no doubt meant conventional and bourgeois.

Flaubert's final work is the story of two uneducated, retired clerks who set off together on a set of adventures in what Flaubert considered this less-than-interesting region. They purchase a hundred acres of farmland outside a village called Chavignolles, where they

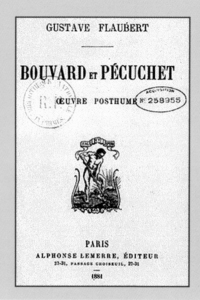

GUSTAVE FLAUBERT

BOUVARD ET PÉCUCHET

ŒUVRE POSTHUME N° 258955

PARIS
ALPHONSE LEMERRE, ÉDITEUR
27-31, PASSAGE CHOISEUIL, 27-31
1881

try their hands at rural life. Over a period of more than twenty years, the two buffoons experiment with farming, medicine, and a string of other unsuccessful pursuits.

The novel, which was originally to be called *A Tale of Two Nobodies*, was initially reconstructed by Flaubert's niece, Caroline, from four thousand pages of manuscript. Although he never finished it, Flaubert worked feverishly while he wrote it, reading hundreds of books on arcane topics and trying to assimilate the material into the text. No amount of book learning, he wanted to show, could compensate for the ultimate stupidity of his two antiheroes.

Flaubert had little expectation that *Bouvard and Pécuchet* would be a popular success.

unforgivable, is that Rouen, all of Rouen did not follow the body of one of its most illustrious children," Zola wrote. "Along the quays, then along the main avenue, clusters of bourgeois watched us curiously, not knowing who the dead man was, or associating the name Flaubert with his father and brother. The truth is that on the event of his death Flaubert was unknown to four-fifths of Rouen and detested by the other fifth."

Zola exaggerated perhaps, but his comments reflect the ambivalence that the writer and his native city felt for one another. Rouen did come to appreciate Flaubert and later chose to honor him with statues and street names, but the relationship remains complex. The few possessions he left are now scattered around the old Norman capital and its environs. Some are on display at the Croisset pavilion, which remains as an island in Rouen's industrial outskirts, while others are carefully

preserved in the hospital that was his childhood home. His manuscripts and photographs are carefully filed away in Rouen's main library, while his own library of roughly eight hundred volumes is stacked in its original bookshelves several miles away at Canteleu's modern town hall. And in the Rouen suburb of Mont-Saint-Aignan, Flaubert scholars have catalogued his work and correspondence on a website devoted to the writer.

In the many decades since the trail of devoted friends and family made their way to Rouen's hilltop cemetery, Flaubert's legacy has expanded far beyond his native province. The University of Rouen's website offers links to translations and critiques from Hungary, China, and beyond. Modern literary critics credit him with writing the first "modern" novel, one that refuses to judge its characters and seeks to tell the truth in painstaking detail, even as its author leaves little trace.

In the end, however, Flaubert did leave a lasting trace—one that influenced the course of twentieth-century literature and culture in France and far beyond. "Novelists should thank Gustave Flaubert the way poets thank spring: it begins again with him," wrote James Wood, a professor of literary criticism at Harvard University, in a *New York Times* review of Frederick Brown's *Flaubert: A Biography*. Wood pointed out that Flaubert, as the originator of modern narrative, influenced not only the writers who came just after him, such as Marcel Proust and James Joyce, but also modern twentieth-century writers. His pair of buffoons in *Bouvard and Pécuchet*—the clerks who set off on a series of absurd quests—set the stage for Vladimir and Estragon, the two tramps in *Waiting for Godot*, Samuel Beckett's absurdist play first performed—in Paris—in 1953. Flaubert's obsession with style and rhythm also helped to change the course of modern literature. For example, the French writers Alain Robbe-Grillet and Nathalie Sarraute—creators of the Nouveau Roman (new novel) movement, which sought to elevate minimalist style over traditional attention to plot and characters—credited Flaubert for first dreaming of writing "a book about nothing."

Indeed, Flaubert went to great lengths to distance himself from the Normandy subject and

Flaubert's statue stands today in Place des Carmes in central Rouen, the city where he was born but which ignored him during his lifetime.

setting of his most famous writing. In the midst of composing *Madame Bovary* in June 1853, he wrote to Louise Colet about the relative unimportance of his subject:

> If the book I am writing with such difficulty turns out well, I'll have established, by the very fact of having written it, these two truths, which for me are axiomatic, namely: (1) that poetry is purely subjective, that in literature there are no such things as beautiful subjects, and that therefore Yvetot (a Normandy town) is the equal of Constantinople; and (2) that consequently one can write about any one thing equally well as about any other.

In the end, however, Flaubert never succeeded in cutting himself off from Normandy: its green hills and farmland, windswept beaches, and bourgeois society nurtured his imagination even as they riled his sensibilities. "The artist must raise everything to a higher level: he is like a pump; he has inside him a great pipe that reaches down into the entrails of things, the deepest layers," he continued in his letter to Colet. "He sucks up what was lying there below, dim and unnoticed, and brings it out in great jets to the sunlight."

Timeline

1821 — Gustave Flaubert is born in Rouen at the Hôtel Dieu (municipal hospital). He is the second son of Achille-Cléophas Flaubert, chief surgeon at the Hôtel Dieu, and Anne-Caroline Fleuriot, daughter of a physician from Pônt-l'Evêque. The Flauberts already have a son, Achille, born in 1813, and in 1824 they have a daughter, Caroline. Three other children, born between 1813 and 1824, die as infants.

1825 — A servant girl nicknamed Julie comes to work for the Flaubert family. She dotes on the young Gustave and serves as the inspiration late in his life for the character of Félicité in his short story "A Simple Heart." Flaubert keeps in touch with Julie throughout his life, and she returns to visit him as an old lady and outlives him.

1832 — Flaubert starts school at the Collège Royal de Rouen as a boarder.

1835–39 — The family spends summer vacations at Trouville, then an out-of-the-way fishing village on the Channel coast.

1836 — Flaubert has his first meeting with Elisa Schlesinger on a Trouville beach. He develops a hopeless passion for the young mother.

1838 — He writes his first novel,

Memoirs of a Madman, based on meeting Elisa, which later serves as a preliminary sketch for *Sentimental Education*.

1839 — Flaubert is expelled from school because of his leadership of a student protest. He passes his final examinations at home.

1840 — Flaubert voyages to Corsica with a family friend. On the way he meets Eulalie Foucaud in a Marseilles hotel and has his first consummated amorous encounter. (He had visited Rouen brothels before the meeting.)

1842 — Flaubert moves to Paris to begin law studies. He passes his first-year exams but fails the second-year test the following year. He likes Paris, but the legal studies bore him.

1843 — He meets Maxime Du Camp, who will become a close friend, and starts work on the first version of *Sentimental Education*.

1844 — Flaubert suffers his first "nervous attack," now thought to be

A drawing of Flaubert as a boy by his brother, Achille.

The town of Ry claims to be the real Yonville, the dull and censorious provincial town where Emma Bovary meets her fate.

an epileptic seizure, while traveling with his brother to Pont-l'Evêque. In April of the same year, Dr. Flaubert buys a house at Croisset, and in June the family moves there. Flaubert abandons his legal studies and moves permanently to Croisset.

1845 — Flaubert's younger sister, Caroline, marries Emile Hamard, a former classmate of Flaubert's.

1846 — Dr. Flaubert dies in January. In March Caroline dies two months after giving birth to a daughter, also named Caroline.

1846–54 — Flaubert has a tempestuous, on-again-off-again affair with the poet Louise Colet.

1849–51 — He travels to southern Europe and the Middle East with friend Maxime Du Camp.

1851 — Shortly after returning to Croisset, Flaubert starts work on *Madame Bovary*.

1856 — *Madame Bovary* is published in serial form in a literary journal.

1857 — Flaubert goes on trial for writing an immoral book. He is acquitted and *Madame Bovary* is published in book form and is a great success.

1858 — Flaubert travels to Carthage and North Africa to do research for his book *Salammbô*.

1862 — Flaubert finishes *Salammbô* after months of hard work in isolation at Croisset.

1863 — Start of friendship with George Sand. Flaubert also meets Ivan Turgenev for the first time.

1864 — Flaubert persuades his niece, Caroline, to marry Ernest Commanville, a lumber dealer whom she does not love.

Honfleur, where Flaubert's mother attended boarding school and where Félicité, the heroine of "A Simple Heart," takes her parrot to be stuffed.

1869 — Flaubert publishes *Sentimental Education*, which receives generally negative reviews.

1870 — France declares war on Prussia in July. In December, victorious Prussian troops arrive in Rouen.

1872 — Flaubert's mother dies.

1874 — *The Temptation of Saint Anthony* is published.

1875 — Flaubert's health declines, probably because of syphilis, and he faces serious financial difficulties after Ernest Commanville loses his money. Flaubert agrees to help bail him out by selling his only property, a farm in Deauville that was Flaubert's chief source of income.

1876 — Flaubert travels to Pont l'Evêque and Honfleur in preparation for writing the short story "A Simple Heart." The trip makes him melancholy and nostalgic for his youth. Later that year, George Sand dies before he has completed his story, which he was writing in part to please her.

1877 — *Three Tales* is published to widespread acclaim.

1880 — Flaubert dies at his house in Croisset, leaving his last novel, *Bouvard and Pécuchet*, unfinished.

The white tombstones of Flaubert (on left) and his sister Caroline (right) flank those of their parents.

Notes

Unless otherwise noted, all translations from the French are by the author.

Chapter 1

3: "Be regular and orderly in your life . . .": A widely quoted Flaubert maxim, www.theotherpages.org/unsort13.html.

4: "Oh how I'd rather live in Spain . . .": Flaubert, letter to Ernest Chevalier, 1840, www.univ-rouen.fr/flaubert.

4: "Sometimes I think I'm liquefying . . .": Flaubert, letter to niece Caroline, April 28, 1880, univ-rouen.fr/flaubert.

5: "If my book is any good it will tickle many a feminine wound . . .": Flaubert, quoted in Geoffrey Wall, *Flaubert: A Life* (New York: Farrar, Straus and Giroux, 2001), 202.

6: Flaubert felt "a torrent of flames . . .": Flaubert, quoted in Wall, *Flaubert*, 79.

6: "My illness has brought one benefit . . .": Flaubert, letter to Emmanuel Vasse de Saint-Ouen, January 1845, *The Letters of Gustave Flaubert, 1830–1857*, selected, edited, and translated by Francis Steegmuller (Cambridge, MA, and London: Belknap Press of Harvard University Press, 1979), 23.

7: "Why I have stayed . . ."; Flaubert, letter to Maxime Du Camp, October 24, 1841, *Letters, 1830–1857*, 148.

7: "I live alone like a bear . . .": Flaubert, letter to Emmanuel Vasse de Saint-Ouen, *Letters, 1830–1857*, 23.

10: "It seems that calamity is upon us . . .": Flaubert, letter to Maxime Du Camp, March 15, 1846, *Letters, 1830–1857*, 37.

10: "I hate Europe, France . . .": Flaubert, letter to Ernest Chevalier, November 14, 1840, *Letters, 1830–1857*, 13.

10: "What a heavy oar the pen is . . .": Flaubert, letter to Louise Colet, October 23, 1851, *Letters, 1830–1857*, 151.

10: "It is strange how I was born . . .": Flaubert, letter to Louise Colet, April 7, 1846, www.univ-rouen.fr/flaubert.

11: "liberty but not power . . .": George Sand, *Letters, 1830–1857*, 183.

12: "Perhaps race wars . . .": Flaubert, letter to George Sand, August 3, 1870, *Letters, 1830–1857*, 155.

12: "My poor dear Mother . . .": Flaubert, letter to George Sand, April 16, 1872, www.univ-rouen.fr/flaubert.

Chapter 2

16: "Then, all at once, the city came into view . . .":
Gustave Flaubert, *Madame Bovary*, translated by Francis
Steegmuller (New York: Random House for Modern
Library, 1957), 299.

15: "To her the old Norman city was like some fabulous
capital . . .": Flaubert, *Madame Bovary*, 299.

15: "beautiful churches and stupid inhabitants . . .":
Flaubert, letter to Ernest Chevalier, September 2, 1843,
www.univ-rouen.fr/flaubert.

19: "What is fame! . . .": Flaubert, letter to Louise
Colet, November 7, 1847, *Letters, 1830–1857*, 92.

20: "Everything changes, even stone": Claude Monet,
www.getty.edu/art/gettyguide/artObjectDetails?artobj=1
42049.

22: "One of the most beautiful trade routes . . .": From
an ancient Greek geographer, Strabo, press kit from the
City of Rouen.

22: "five feet nine inches tall, with brown eyes . . .":
Flaubert, quoted in Wall, *Flaubert*, 13.

22: "This great, ugly, stinking, close and ill-built
town . . .": Arthur Young, *Travels in France*,
www.econlib.org/library/YPDBooks/Young/yngTF3.html.

22: Information on the Reign of Terror in Rouen is
from a review of Gavin Daly, *Inside Napoleonic France:
State and Society in Rouen* www.napoleon-series.org/
reviews/ general/c_daly.html.

23: "The high deeds which continue . . .": Flaubert,
quoted in Wall, *Flaubert*, 14.

25: "I'm writing with an 'Amazon'. . .": Flaubert, quoted
in Wall, *Flaubert*, 38.

25: "Why does the writing make us chase the
writer? . . .": Julian Barnes, *Flaubert's Parrot* (New York:
Vintage Books, 1984), 12.

25: "I have no biography . . .": Flaubert, letter to Ernest
Feydeau, August 21, 1859, www.univ-rouen.fr/flaubert

26: Information about Rouen's public library comes
from Herbert Lottman, *Flaubert: A Biography* (New
York: Fromm International Publishing Corporation,
1990), 9.

26: "One of France's most important doctors . . .":
Pierre Berteau, "Docteur Achille-Cléophas Flaubert,"
Bulletin Flaubert, No. 15 (2004), 230.

26: "send my heart . . .": Flaubert, letter to George
Sand, quoted in Wall, *Flaubert*, 21.

29: "We warmed ourselves lazily . . .": Flaubert, quoted
in Wall, *Flaubert*, 36.

29: "We were in study hall . . .": Flaubert, *Madame
Bovary*, 3.

31: Information on Flaubert's interest in antiquity
comes from *The Cambridge Companion to Flaubert*,
edited by Timothy Unwin (Cambridge: Cambridge
University Press), 86.

31: "If you want to hear some news . . .": Flaubert,
letter to Ernest Chevalier, quoted in Wall, *Flaubert*, 36.

31: "Half my brain . . .": Flaubert, quoted in *Auteurs
Francais Contemporains*, www.alalettre.com/
flaubert-intro.htm.

32: "Here was a man . . .": Flaubert, in "Lettre de M. Gustave Flaubert à la Municipalité de Rouen," perso.orange.fr/jb.guinot/pages/flaurouen.html.

33: "He [Flaubert] would go for months on end . . .": Caroline Franklin Grout, *Souvenirs Intimes (Intimate Memories)*, www.univ-rouen.fr/flaubert.

34: "I have the poet who with a tearful eye . . .": Louis Bouilhet, quoted in Guy de Maupassant, *Found on a Drowned Man* (The Classical Library, 2001), www.classicallibrary.org/maupassant/ossv8/6.htm.

34: "It is truly wrong . . .": Flaubert, letter to Alfred Le Poittevin, April 2, 1845, *Letters, 1830–1857*, 24.

34: "I am still prostrated by this calamity . . .": Guy de Maupassant, letter to Ivan Turgenev, May 25, 1880, *Letters, 1830–1857*, 275.

35: "I'm impatient to tell you . . .": Flaubert, letter to Guy de Maupassant, February 1, 1880, *Letters, 1830–1857*, 265.

37: "I arrived in Rouen at one o'clock . . .": George Sand, letter to Flaubert, in *Flaubert-Sand: The Correspondence*, translated by Francis Steegmuller and Barbara Bray (New York: Alfred A. Knopf, 1993), 17.

38: "The church was like a gigantic boudoir . . .": Flaubert, *Madame Bovary*, 273.

38: "Anywhere . . .": Flaubert, *Madame Bovary*, 278.

39: "And there is the story . . .": Gustave Flaubert, *Three Tales*, translated by Roger Whitehouse (New York: Penguin Classics, 2005), 70.

39: "Then she began to dance . . .": Flaubert, *Three Tales*, 100.

Chapter 3

43: "In my youth I loved immeasurably . . .": Flaubert, letter to Amélie Bosquet, 1859, www.univ-rouen.fr/flaubert.

44: "She was tall, dark . . .": Gustave Flaubert, *Les Mémoires d'un Fou* (Paris: Gallimard, 2001), 73.

44: "I cannot take a step . . .": Francis Steegmuller, *Flaubert and Madame Bovary* (Boston: Houghton Mifflin Company, 1970), 289.

45: Information about nineteenth-century brothels comes from Francine du Plessix Gray, *Rage and Fire: A Life of Louise Colet* (New York: Simon & Schuster, 1994), 128–129.

45: "I love prostitution for itself . . .": Flaubert, letter to Louise Colet, June 1, 1853, www.univ-rouen.fr/flaubert.

45: "Syphilis: Everybody has it, more or less": Gustave Flaubert, *The Dictionary of Accepted Ideas*, translated by Jacques Barzun (New York: New Directions, 1954), 84.

45: "Living for oneself . . .": George Sand, letter to Flaubert, *Flaubert-Sand*, 285.

46: "I scarcely shut my eyes . . .": Flaubert, letter to Louis Bouilhet, March 13, 1850, *Letters, 1830–1857*, 116.

47: "He was not a man . . .": Flaubert, letter to Louise Colet, September 25, 1852, *Letters, 1830–1857*, 171.

47: "His perpetual state of fluctuation . . .": Steegmuller, *Letters, 1830–1857*, 190.

48: "They almost always rested on the same field . . .": Flaubert, *Three Tales*, 12.

49: "The road was so bad . . .": Flaubert, *Three Tales*, 11.

50: "In the afternoon . . .": Flaubert, *Three Tales*, 12.

51: "At other times . . .": Flaubert, *Three Tales*, 13.

52: "At the time Gustave Flaubert looked like. . .": Gertrude Tenant, quoted in *Letters, 1830–1857*, 59.

52: "One day we were alone . . .": Flaubert, letter to Louise Colet, September 22, 1846, *Letters, 1830–1857*, 79.

52: "Women figure very little . . .": Flaubert, letter to Gertrude Collier, *Letters, 1830–1857*, 263.

53: "I had only one true passion . . .": Flaubert, letter to Louise Colet, October 8, 1846, *Letters, 1830–1857*, 84.

53: "For me, the sand on Trouville beach . . .": Flaubert, letter to Elisa Schlesinger, *Letters, 1830–1857*, 194.

53: "I can never see your handwriting . . .": Flaubert, letter to Elisa Schlesinger, October 5, 1872, *Letters, 1830–1857*, 195.

54: "If I have become a painter . . .": Monet, quoted in *Apollo* magazine, "Impressions of Normandy," August 2004.

56: "I spent an hour . . .": Flaubert, letter to Louise Colet, August 14, 1853, *Letters, 1830–1857*, 195.

56: "Twenty five autumn skies . . .": Gustave Courbet, quoted on the Walker Art Gallery, Liverpool, England, website, www.liverpoolmuseums.org.uk.

57: "I admire Flaubert greatly . . .": Marcel Proust, in "A propos de 'style' de Flaubert," which first appeared in *La Nouvelle Revue Française* in 1920, perso.orange.fr/jb.guinot/pages/Proust.html.

59: "The most exciting event . . .": Flaubert, *Three Tales*, 13.

60: "As she came to the top of the hill . . .": Flaubert, *Three Tales*, 33.

Chapter 4

67: "Back in my cave . . .": Flaubert, letter to Alfred Le Poittevin, June 17, 1845, *Letters, 1830–1857*, 34.

67: "The sky is clear, the moon is shining . . .": Flaubert, letter to Louise Colet, August 8–9, 1846, *Letters, 1830–1857*, 50.

68: "The crowd was growing steadily . . .": Gustave Flaubert, *Sentimental Education*, translated by Robert Baldick (London: Penguin Books, 1964), 276.

69: "The man who retains the same self-esteem . . .": Flaubert, letter to Louis Bouilhet, November 14, 1850, *Letters, 1830–1857*, 130.

69: "My mother claims that I've changed . . .": Flaubert, quoted in Wall, *Flaubert*, 190.

69: "Monstrosity . . .": Flaubert, letter to his mother, December 15, 1850, *Letters, 1830–1857*, 132.

70: "I've just passed a week alone like a hermit . . .": Flaubert, letter to Louis Bouilhet, August 18, 1854, www.univ-rouen.fr/flaubert.

70: "We got to Croisset at half-past three . . .": George Sand, in *Flaubert-Sand*, 17.

71: "Bouilhet was here Friday night . . .": Flaubert, letter to Louise Colet, January 2, 1854, *Letters, 1830–1857*, 207.

71: "After breakfast we went for a walk . . .": George Sand, in *Flaubert-Sand*, 32.

72: "It is impossible for Monsieur . . .": Steegmuller, *Letters, 1830–1857*, 142.

72: "O bed! . . .": Louise Colet, quoted in Wall, *Flaubert*, 114.

72: "A gift from Louise Colet . . .": du Plessix Gray, *Rage and Fire*, 83.

72: "You think that you will love me for ever . . .": Flaubert, letter to Louise Colet, August 6 or 7, 1846, *Letters, 1830–1857*, 47.

73: "Madame: . . .": Flaubert, letter to Louise Colet, March 6, 1855, *Letters, 1830–1857*, 215.

73: "As I went up the hill at Canteleu . . .": Guy de Maupassant, *The Gamekeeper*, translated by Albert M. C. McMaster, A. E. Henderson, Mme. Quesada, et al., classiclit.about.com/library/bl-etexts/gdemaupassant/bl-gdemaup-gamekeeper.htm.

77: "They cut down the apple trees . . .": Wall, *Flaubert*, 347.

78: "With only a few day's notice . . .": Caroline Commanville, letter to Edma Roger des Genettes, *Letters, 1830–1857*, 299.

79: "Flaubert, impassioned and more sympathetic . . .": George Sand, quoted in *Letters, 1830–1857*, 86.

Chapter 5

83: "That is as much as there is to see . . .": Flaubert, *Madame Bovary*, 83.

84: "I used no model . . .": Flaubert, letter to Mademoiselle Leroyer de Chantepie, March 18, 1857, www.univ-rouen.fr/flaubert.

85: "Last night I began my novel . . .": Flaubert, letter to Louise Colet, September 20, 1851, *Letters, 1830–1857*, 145.

85: "For two days now . . .": Flaubert, letter to Louise Colet, March 3, 1852, *Letters, 1830–1857*, 156.

86: Quotations about Emma's appearance are from *Madame Bovary*.

87: "It is splendid to be a great writer . . .": Flaubert, letter to Louise Colet, November 3, 1851, *Letters, 1830–1857*, 152.

88: "Since two o'clock yesterday . . .": Flaubert, letter to Louise Colet, December 23, 1853, *Letters 1830–1857*, 203.

88: "Smoked three pipes . . .": Flaubert, *Madame Bovary*, 230.

88: "My wretched novel . . .": Flaubert, letter to Louis Bouilhet, September 1855, *Letters, 1830–1857*, 217.

88: "At any moment . . .": Flaubert, letter to brother Achille, January 1857, *Letters, 1830–1857*, 223.

89: "Maitre Sénard's speech . . .": Flaubert, letter to brother Achille, January 30, 1857, *Letters, 1830–1857*, 226.

89: "Antoine-Marie-Jules Sénard . . .": Letter to Maitre Sénard, classiclit.about.com/library/bl-etexts/gflaubert/bl-gflau-mbovaryded.htm.

90: "The son and brother of eminent doctors . . .": Charles Augustin Sainte-Beuve, *Selected Essays* (Garden City, NY: Doubleday & Company, Inc., 1957), 290.

90: "Madam Bovary, c'est moi . . .": Flaubert, in Steegmuller, *Flaubert and Madame Bovary*, 283.

90: "My poor Bovary . . .": Flaubert, letter to Louise Colet, September 1855, www.univ-rouen.fr/flaubert.

90: "Show more clearly than all of the critics . . .": Discussion of the debate comes from Jean-Marie Privat, Emma à Ry. "Notes de recherche," ethnographiques.org, No. 5 (April 2004).

90: "Gustavus Flaubertus . . .": Quoted from Peter Gay, *The Pleasure Wars: The Bourgeois Experience* (New York: W. W. Norton & Co. Inc., 1998).

90: "The devil himself doesn't have a greater following . . .": Flaubert, *Madame Bovary*, 396.

93: "Then, late in September . . .": Flaubert, *Madame Bovary*, 51.

94: "At the end of the village . . .": Description of Yonville-l'Abbaye is from *Madame Bovary*, Part Two, Chapter 1.

96: "Flaubert had a cinematographic mind . . .": Claude Chabrol, quoted in *Telegraph* magazine, August 31, 1991.

Chapter 6

103: "Eight days ago I made a sad trip . . .": Flaubert, letter to Caroline Commanville, June 28–29, 1870, www.univ-rouen.fr/flaubert.

103: "So I live alone . . .": Flaubert, letter to Edmond de Goncourt, June 26, 1870, *Letters, 1857–1880*, 149.

104: "I feel we are entering black darkness . . .": Flaubert, letter to George Sand, August 3, 1870, *The Letters of Gustave Flaubert, 1857–1880*, selected, edited, and translated by Francis Steegmuller (Cambridge, MA, and London; Belknap Press of Harvard University Press, 1982), 155.

104: "All day I saw the bayonets . . .": Flaubert, letter to Princesse Mathilde, March 4, 1870, *Letters, 1857–1880*, 169.

104: "Contrary to my expectations . . .": Flaubert, letter to Caroline Commanville, April 4, 1871, *Letters, 1857–1880*, 173.

105: "Write something more down to earth . . .": Flaubert, letter to George Sand, October 8, 1875, *Letters, 1857–1880*, 222.

105: "This excursion plunged me into melancholy . . .":
Flaubert, letter to Edma Roger des Genettes, 1876,
Letters, 1857–1880, 234.

105: "Before dinner, around seven . . .": Flaubert,
letter to Guy de Maupassant, 1876, www.univ-rouen.fr/
flaubert.

105: "In the night the sentences go rolling . . .":
Flaubert, letter to Caroline Commanville, 1876,
www.univ-rouen.fr/flaubert.

106: "I do not address these remarks . . .": Flaubert,
Sentimental Education, in *Flaubert-Sand*, 3.

106: "I began A Simple Heart exclusively for her . . .":
Flaubert, letter to Maurice Sand, August 28, 1877,
Letters, 1857–1880, 239.

106: "I was burying my mother . . .": Flaubert, letter to
Maurice Sand, quoted in Wall, *Flaubert*, 337.

106: "One had to know her . . .": Flaubert, letter to
Mademoiselle Leroyer de Chantepie, June 17, 1876,
quoted in *Flaubert-Sand*, 234.

107: "is quite simply the tale of the obscure life . . .":
Flaubert, quoted in Frederick Brown, *Flaubert: A
Biography* (Boston: Little, Brown & Co., 2006), 516.

108: "With a slate roof . . .": description of Pont-
l'Evêque from Flaubert, *Three Tales*, 3–5.

110: "Genuflecting as she went through the door . . .":
Flaubert, *Three Tales*, 14.

112: Information on the Geffosses Farm is from Pierre-
Jean Pénault, *Personnage et décors dans Un Coeur Simple
de Gustave Flaubert*, a pamphlet published by the
tourism office, Pont-l'Evêque.

112: "Whenever the weather was fine . . .": Flaubert,
Three Tales, 9.

113: "The death of our poor Mme. Sand . . .": Flaubert,
letter to Ivan Turgenev, June 25, 1876, *Letters,
1857–1880*, 235.

114: "*Bouvard and Pécuchet* keeps trotting along . . .":
Flaubert, letter to Guy de Maupassant, August 1878,
Letters, 1857–1880, 243.

114: "I satisfy my need for affection . . .": Flaubert,
letter to Caroline Commanville, 1879,
www.univ-rouen.fr/flaubert.

115: Information on Flaubert's falling out with Edmond
Laporte is from *Letters, 1857–1880*, 256.

115: "Princes have always given such things . . .": Guy
de Maupassant, letter to Flaubert, March 7, 1879,
Letters, 1857–1880, 257.

115: "I have the honor to inform you . . .": Jules Ferry,
letter to Flaubert, October 3, 1879, *Letters, 1857–1880*,
262.

115: "The enormously wide Seine . . .": Edmond de
Goncourt, March 28, 1880, journal entry, *Letters,
1857–1880*, 270.

116: "Which had Flaubert shaking with laughter . . .":
Edmond de Goncourt, quoted in Brown, *Flaubert: A
Biography*, 556.

116: "I've got to the point . . .": Flaubert, letter to Ivan Turgenev, April 7, 1880, *Letters, 1857–1880*, 272.

116: Circumstances of Flaubert's death are from Wall, *Flaubert*, 344.

116: "The death of Gustave Flaubert hit us like a lightning bolt . . .": Emile Zola, http://perso.orange.fr/jb.guinot/pages/flauzola. html.

117: "Stupid plateau . . .": Flaubert, letter to Caroline Commanville, June 24, 1874, in Brown, *Flaubert: A Biography*, 539.

118: "Novelists should thank Gustave Flaubert the way poets thank spring . . .": James Wood, in an April 16, 2006, *New York Times* review of Frederick Brown's *Flaubert: A Biography*, nytimes.com.

118: "If the book I am writing with such difficulty turns out well . . .": Flaubert, letter to Louise Colet, June 25, 1853, *Letters, 1857–1880*, 189.

118: "The artist must raise everything . . .": Flaubert, letter to Louise Colet, June 25, 1853, *Letters, 1857–1880*, 189.

For Further Reading

Writings by Gustave Flaubert

The Letters of Gustave Flaubert, 1830–1857. Selected, edited, and translated by Francis Steegmuller. Cambridge, MA, and London: Belknap Press of Harvard University Press, 1979.

The Letters of Gustave Flaubert, 1857–1880. Selected, edited, and translated by Francis Steegmuller. Cambridge, MA, and London: Belknap Press of Harvard University Press, 1982.

Flaubert-Sand, The Correspondence. Translated by Francis Steegmuller and Barbara Bray. New York: Alfred A. Knopf, 1993.

Flaubert, Gustave. *Madame Bovary*. Translated by Francis Steegmuller. New York: The Modern Library, 1950.

———. *Sentimental Education*. Translated by Robert Baldick. London and New York: Penguin, 1964.

———. *Three Tales*. Translated by Roger Whitehouse. London and New York: Penguin, 2005.

———. *Salammbo*. Translated by A. L. Krailsheimer. Middlesex, England and New York: Penguin, 1977.

———. *A Dictionary of Accepted Ideas*. Translated by Jacques Barzun. New York: New Directions, 1954.

Biographies and Critical Studies

Barnes, Julian. *Something to Declare: Essays on France and French Culture*. New York: Vintage, 2003.

Brown, Frederick. *Flaubert: A Biography*. Boston: Little, Brown & Co., 2006.

Du Plessix Gray, Francine, *Rage and Fire: A Life of Louise Colet*. New York: Simon & Schuster, 1994.

Lottman, Herbert. *Flaubert: A Biography*. New York: Fromm International Publishing Corporation, 1990.

Perry, K. R. *The Bourgeois Century: A History of Europe, 1780-1870*. New York: Humanities Press, 1972.

Sainte-Beuve, Charles. *The Collected Essays*. Translated and edited by Francis Steegmuller and Norbert Guterman. Garden City, NY: Doubleday & Company, 1993.

Steegmuller, Francis. *Flaubert and Madame Bovary*. Boston: Houghton Mifflin, 1970.

Troyat, Henri. *Flaubert*. Translated by Joan Pinkham. New York: Viking Penguin, 1992.

Wall, Geoffrey. *Flaubert: A Life*. New York: Farrar, Straus and Giroux, 2001.

Other Books of Interest

Barnes, Julian. *Flaubert's Parrot*. New York: Vintage, 1990.

Bentley, James. *Normandy*. London: Aurum, 1989.

Insight Guide: Normandy. London: APA Publications, 2000.

Web Resources

Le Site Flaubert is maintained by the Flaubert Center at the University of Rouen in partnership with the Bibliothèque Municipale de Rouen. The site offers a wide array of documents and information about Flaubert, his writing, and his contemporaries. It includes access to Flaubert's correspondence online: www.univ-rouen.fr/Flaubert/.

The Gustave Flaubert site: perso.wanadoo.fr/jb.guinot/pages/accueil.html.

Index

Credits

Image on page 86, *Rigolette Seeking to Distract Herself during the Absence of Germain, from Eugene Sue's Novel "Les mysteres de Paris"* (1844), Edward Court; Erich Lessing/Art Resource, NY.

Image on page 99 is courtesy of Erich Lessing / Art Resource, NY.

Images on page 104 [LC-DIG-pga-02713], page 105 [LC-USZ62-128230], and page 116 [LC-USZ62-105941] are from the U.S. Library of Congress Prints and Photographs Division.

Image on page 113 is courtesy Madame Jacquelet.

Image on page 115, *Emile Zola* (1868), Edouard Manet; Erich Lessing/Art Resource, NY.

All other images are in the public domain or from the author's collection.

About the Author

Susannah Patton grew up in San Francisco, but her interest in things French began early with school classes and a high school summer in France. She spent her junior year in Paris while majoring in French literature at Carleton College and then returned to Paris to live for three years. During this time she studied political science at the Insitut d'Etudes Politiques and worked as a journalist for the *International Herald Tribune*. Later, after earning a graduate degree in journalism from Columbia University, she returned to Paris as a reporter, first for Dow Jones and subsequently for the Associated Press. While in Paris, she also wrote stories for *Time* magazine, the *Dallas Morning News*, and the *Baltimore Sun*. She is a former senior writer for *CIO* magazine. During her last two years in France, she spent weekends with her husband and two young sons at a farm cottage in Normandy, cementing her appreciation of Flaubert's life and work. She now lives with her family in Albany, California.

About the ArtPlace Series

This book is part of the ArtPlace series published by Roaring Forties Press. Each book in the series explores how a renowned artist and a world-famous city or area helped to define and inspire each other. ArtPlace volumes are intended to stimulate both eye and mind, offering a rich mix of art and photography, history and biography, ideas and information. While the books can be used by tourists to navigate and illuminate their way through cityscapes and landscapes, the volumes can also be read by armchair travelers in search of an engrossing and revealing story.

Titles include *A Journey into Dorothy Parker's New York, A Journey into Steinbeck's California, A Journey into the Transcendentalists' New England, A Journey into Matisse's South of France, A Journey into Ireland's Literary Revival, A Journey into Michelangelo's Rome,* and *A Journey into Georgia O'Keeffe's New Mexico.*

Visit Roaring Forties Press's website, www.roaringfortiespress.com, for details of these and other forthcoming titles, as well as to learn about upcoming author tours, readings, media appearances, and all kinds of special events and offers. Visitors to the website may also send comments and questions to the authors of ArtPlace series books.

A Journey into Flaubert's Normandy

This book is set in Goudy and Futura; the display type is Futura Condensed. The interior and cover of the book were designed by Jeff Urbancic. Susan Lynch made up the pages. Nigel Quinney and Sherri Schultz edited the text, which was proofread by Jill Marts Lodwig and indexed by Jan Williams.